AN ANALYSIS OF STATUTORY LAWS GOVERNING COMMERCIAL AND EDUCATIONAL BROADCASTING IN THE FIFTY STATES

This is a volume in the
Arno Press collection

DISSERTATIONS IN BROADCASTING

Advisory Editor
Christopher H. Sterling

See last pages of this volume
for a complete list of titles.

AN ANALYSIS OF STATUTORY LAWS GOVERNING COMMERCIAL AND EDUCATIONAL BROADCASTING IN THE FIFTY STATES

Robert Paul Sadowski

ARNO PRESS
A New York Times Company
New York • 1979

Editorial Supervision: Andrea Hicks

First publication 1979 by Arno Press Inc.

DISSERTATIONS IN BROADCASTING
ISBN for complete set: 0-405-11754-X
See last pages of this volume for titles.

Manufactured in the United States of America

Library of Congress Cataloging in Publication Data

Sadowski, Robert Paul.
An analysis of statutory laws governing commercial and educational broadcasting in the fifty states.

(Dissertations in broadcasting)
Originally presented as the author's thesis, University of Iowa, 1973.
Bibliography: p.
1. Broadcasting--Law and legislation--United States--States. I. Title. II. Series.
KF2805.Z95S33 1979 343'.73'0994 78-21736
ISBN 0-405-11773-6

AN ANALYSIS OF STATUTORY LAWS GOVERNING COMMERCIAL AND EDUCATIONAL BROADCASTING IN THE FIFTY STATES

by

Robert Paul Sadowski

A thesis submitted in partial fulfillment of the
requirements for the degree of Doctor of Philosophy
in the Department of Speech and Dramatic Art
in the Graduate College of
The University of Iowa

May, 1973

Thesis supervisor: Professor Samuel L. Becker

ACKNOWLEDGMENTS

I wish to express my sincere appreciation to Dr. Samuel L. Becker for his invaluable assistance with this dissertation and for his encouragement and support throughout my doctoral studies.

I am also grateful to the other members of my dissertation committee: Dr. Anthony Adams, Dr. Hugh Cordier, Dr. Douglas Ehninger, and Dr. Hanno Hardt.

I also wish to acknowledge the valuable assistance given me by the library staff at the University of Iowa College of Law.

Finally, I thank my wife Barbara whose constant help and encouragement made this dissertation possible.

TABLE OF CONTENTS

LIST OF TABLES

CHAPTER I

A LEGAL RATIONALE FOR STATE REGULATION OF BROADCASTING

Broadcast regulation research has traditionally dealt with federal laws.[1] This emphasis is understandable because radio and television broadcasting is in or affects interstate commerce and, consequently, is regulated by a federal agency, namely the Federal Communications Commission. Since broadcast regulation is primarily a federal matter it might appear that the states have been ousted from legislating any statutory controls governing broadcast activities. As this chapter will show, though, the states have not been wholly precluded from exercising regulatory controls over certain aspects of broadcasting. Although the legitimacy of state legislation has been clearly established by Congress and the courts, practically nothing is known about which aspects of broadcasting are in fact being regulated by the states. This dissertation is an attempt to remedy this dearth of information by examining all the state statutes which regulate various aspects of broadcasting.

The primary responsibility for the regulation of radio and television broadcasting in the United States is vested in the Federal Communications Commission which enforces the provisions of the Communications Act of 1934.[2] The regulatory provisions of this Act have been judicially determined to be a reasonable exercise of Congressional power.[3] This Congressional power derives from the United States Constitution which delegates to Congress the power "To regulate Commerce with foreign Nations, and among the several States."[4] In adopting the Constitution, it was apparent "from a consideration of the history of the times,"[5] that the people of the states "surrendered certain rights and powers to the central government and, commensurately, diminished the sovereign powers of the state to the extent that such powers were vested in the federal government."[6] Therefore, "when the federal government acts within the limits conferred by the United States Constitution, its action supersedes the powers of the states,"[7] and "a state statute, . . . even if based on the valid police powers of a State, must yield in case of direct conflict with the exercise by the government of the United States of any power it possesses under the Constitution."[8] Therefore,

> Whatever the law of the state, whether embodied in its constitution, statutes, or judicial decisions, the provisions of the federal Constitution and laws are supreme, and the federal Constitution and all laws enacted pursuant to the powers conferred by it on congress are the supreme law of the land to the same extent as though expressly written into every state law.[9]

The Communications Act of 1934 is the supreme law of the land for broadcasting. In enacting this law, Congress stated the purpose of the Communications Act to be that of "regulating interstate and foreign commerce in communication by wire and radio."[10] Furthermore, the definition of "radio communication"[11] has been construed to include television as "one form of radio transmission," and "there can be no doubt of the correctness of this construction."[12]

Since there is no question that Congress has the power to regulate interstate communications vis-a-vis the commerce clause of the U.S. Constitution,[13] and since a federal court noted that "Radio communications are all interstate, . . . though they may be intended only for intrastate transmission,"[14] it might appear that the field has been completely preempted by federal law and that there is no room for the exercise of any state regulation.[15] However, this conclusion is not valid, as a brief review of relevant court decisions and judicial opinions reveals.

The landmark case supporting a state's right to regulate broadcasting was _Head_ v. _New Mexico Board of Examiners in Optometry_ in 1963.[16] The case involved a newspaper and radio station located in Hobbs, New Mexico, a city near the Texas border. Much of the area served by both media is in Texas. The appellants (the newspaper and radio station) were enjoined by a New Mexico State Court from accepting or publishing within the state a Texas optometrist's advertising found to be in violation of a New Mexico state statute that regulates advertising by optometrists. The New Mexico Supreme Court upheld the trial court's injunction. The case was appealed to the U.S. Supreme Court on the grounds that the New Mexico statute imposes an unlawful burden on interstate commerce, and that regulation of radio broadcast advertising has been preempted by federal law.[17] The U.S. Supreme Court rejected both of these contentions and upheld the state statute.

In answering the appellants' contention regarding an unlawful burden on interstate commerce, the U.S. Supreme Court said:

> Without doubt, the appellants' radio station and newspaper are engaged in interstate commerce, and the injunction in this case has unquestionably imposed some restraint upon that commerce. But these facts alone do not add up to an unconstitutional burden on interstate commerce. As we said in Huron Portland Cement Co. v. City of Detroit, 362 U.S. 440, upholding the application of a Detroit smoke abatement ordinance to ships engaged in interstate and international commerce: 'In determining whether the state has imposed an undue burden on interstate commerce, it must be borne in mind that the Constitution when "conferring upon Congress the regulation of commerce, . . . never intended to cut the States off from legislating on all subjects relating to the health, life, and safety of their citizens, though the legislation might indirectly affect the commerce of the country. Legislation, in a great variety of ways, may affect commerce and persons engaged in it without constituting a

regulation of it, within the meaning of the Constitution." Sherlock v. Alling, 93 U.S. 99, 103; Austin v. Tennessee, 179 U.S. 343; Louisville & Nashville R. Co. v. Kentucky, 183 U.S. 503; The Minnesota Rate Cases, 230 U.S. 352; Boston & Maine R. Co. v. Armburg, 285 U.S. 234; Collins v. American Buslines, Inc., 350 U.S. 528.' 362 U.S., at 443-444.

Like the smoke abatement ordinance in the Huron case, the statute here involved is a measure directly addressed to protection of the public health, and the statute thus falls within the most traditional concept of what is compendiously known as the police power. The legitimacy of state legislation in this precise area has been expressly established. Williamson v. Lee Optical Co., 348 U.S. 483. A state law may not be struck down on the mere showing that its administration affects interstate commerce in some way. 'State regulation, based on the police power, which does not discriminate against interstate commerce or operate to disrupt its required uniformity, may constitutionally stand.' Huron Portland Cement Co. v. City of Detroit, supra, at 448.18

Regarding appellants' contention that radio broadcast advertising has been preempted by federal law, the U.S. Supreme Court said:

> We may begin by noting that the validity of this claim cannot be judged by reference to broad statements about the 'comprehensive' nature of federal regulation under the Federal Communications Act. '. . . Statements concerning the "exclusive jurisdiction" of Congress beg the only controversial question: whether Congress intended to make its jurisdiction exclusive.' California v. Zook, 336 U.S. 725, 731. Kelly v. Washington, 302 U.S. 1, 10-13. In areas of the law not inherently requiring national uniformity, our decisions are clear in requiring that state statutes, otherwise valid, must be upheld unless there is found 'such actual conflict between the two schemes of regulation that both cannot stand in the same area, [or] evidence of a congressional design to preempt the field.' Florida Avocado Growers v. Paul, 373 U.S. 132, 141.19

The Court went on to say:

> There has been no showing of any conflict between this state law and the federal regulatory system, or that the state law stands as an obstacle to the full effectiveness of the federal statute. No specific federal regulations even remotely in conflict with the New Mexico law have been called to our attention. The Commission itself has apparently viewed state regulation of advertising as complementing its regulatory function, rather than in any way conflicting with it. As in Colorado Anti-Discrimination Comm'n v. Continental Air Lines, Inc., 372 U.S. 714, at 724, we are satisfied that the state statute 'at least so long as any power the [Commission] may have remains "dormant and unexercised," will not frustrate any part of the purpose of the federal legislation.'[20]

In a lengthy concurring opinion, Mr. Justice Brennan outlined three tests "by which we determine whether federal legislation has displaced state regulation of a given subject matter." The first test asks whether the subject matter is clearly one "by its very nature admitting only of national supervision." To this, Mr. Justice Brennan answered: "Nothing in our decisions which have required particular state regulations to yield to the Communications Act suggests such a view of the regulatory field."[21]

The second test asks whether "there is evidence of congressional intent exclusively to occupy the field." Mr. Justice Brennan said: "Rather than mandate ouster of state regulations, several provisions of the Communications Act suggest a congressional design to leave standing various forms of state regulation, including the form embodied in the New Mexico statute."[22]

The third test asks whether as a practical matter "both regulations can be enforced without impairing the federal superintendence of the field." Mr. Justice Brennan answered in the affirmative and also said:

> The New Mexico law is one designed principally to protect the State's consumers against a local evil by local application to forbid certain forms of advertising in all mass media. Such legislation, whether concerned with the health and safety of consumers, or with their protection against fraud and deception, embodies a traditional state interest of the sort which our decisions have consistently respected. Rice v. Santa Fe Elevator Corp., 331 U.S. 218, 230. Nor is such legislation required to yield simply because it may in some degree restrict the activities of one who holds a federal license. Cf. Huron Portland Cement Co. v. Detroit, 362 U.S. 440, 447-448.
>
> A conclusion that the state regulation is ousted by the federal requires, under this third test, a showing of conflict either in purpose or in operation between the state and federal regulations involved. The contrary of such a showing is made here, for the FCC, in determining whether a licensee's operation has served the public interest, considers whether he has complied with state and local regulations governing advertising--in other words, the Commission accords important deference to the continued operation of state law in this field. Moreover, the National Association of Broadcasters has also consistently counseled obedience to state law on such matters. The Association, in its extensive Codes of Good Practices for both radio and television, unmistakably enjoins each member to 'refuse the facilities of his station to an advertiser where he has good reason to doubt the integrity of the advertiser, the truth of the advertising representations, or the compliance of the advertiser with the spirit and purpose of all applicable legal requirements'; the Television Code, moreover, expressly enjoins: 'Diligence should be exercised to the end that advertising copy accepted . . . complies with pertinent Federal, state and local laws.'[23]

The Head case, then, clearly sets forth the conditions under which the states may exercise their rights to regulate certain aspects of broadcasting. However, it does not stand alone on this matter. Several other decisions have been handed down by the courts that have supported a state's power to regulate certain aspects of broadcasting. For example, a California District Court of Appeal ruled that a state statute which regulates pre-primary advertising endorsements of political candidates does not invade a field that has been preempted by Congress in the Communications Act of 1934.[24] The United States Court of Appeals for the Ninth Circuit affirmed an Hawaii Supreme Court decision that upheld the validity of a tax levy on the gross receipts of a radio station. The tax was held not to be a burden on interstate commerce.[25]

> Not all state taxation is to be condemned because, in some manner, it has an effect upon commerce between the states. . . . A tax may be levied on net income wholly derived from interstate commerce. Non-discriminatory taxation of the instrumentalities of interstate commerce is not prohibited.[26]

In a reversal judgment, the Supreme Court of Ohio held that transmitting equipment purchased in interstate commerce for use by broadcasting stations was subject to a use tax levied by a state's use tax law. As in the Hawaii case, the court held that such a tax was nondiscriminatory and did not constitute a prohibited burden on interstate commerce and thus did not violate the commerce clause of the Federal Constitution.[27]

In addition to court decisions, several Attorneys General opinions have dealt with the subject of state regulation. For example, the Attorney General of Louisiana stated that a broadcasting station located in Louisiana might be held criminally liable for violation of advertising provisions of a state law regulating optometry, despite the fact that the sponsor is a resident of another state.[28] In a 1971 opinion, the Missouri Attorney General noted that his state's prohibition against lotteries can be enforced against broadcasters since it does not conflict with any federal law, and since there is no evidence that Congress had intended to preempt this type of regulation by the states.[29]

The foregoing court decisions and opinions have established precedents whereby states are not wholly precluded from exercising certain regulatory controls of broadcasting and, therefore, the question may be asked: what are the areas of state regulation currently governing commercial and educational radio and television broadcasting in the United States? My dissertation addresses itself to this question. In addition, this dissertation will also consider the following questions to direct the focus of the examination and analysis of the statutes.

1) How general (across states) is each regulation?

2) Are there redundancies in the law? That is, are states currently regulating areas that are covered by federal statutes or federal court decisions?

3) Are there inconsistencies among states on statutes that cover the same topics?

4) Do some state statutes reflect regional patterns? That is to say, are certain kinds of statutes more prevalent in one area of the country than another, e.g., north versus south?

5) Are there signs of contiguous states effects? That is, generally when a state decides to legislate on a particular matter, it first looks to its neighboring states for possible examples of legislation on the same topic. Does broadcast legislation depart from this customary practice, or are there contiguous states effects? This question overlaps somewhat with the regionalism factor in question # 4.

6) Do some states appear to play the role of "leader" or "innovator" in broadcast legislation? Is there a pattern to the order in which states legislate?

7) Do some states have a law in certain areas that could serve as a model for other states to adopt? Obviously, state laws differ on the same topic. The question is whether they should and whether the law of one particular state is such that all other states should be urged to adopt it.

FOOTNOTES

[1]For example, see Walter B. Emery, *Broadcasting and Government: Responsibilities and Regulations* (East Lansing: Michigan State University Press, 1971).

[2]47 U.S.C.A. Sec. 151 et seq. (1962).

[3]*Pulitzer Pub. Co.* v. *Federal Communications Commission*, 94 F.2d 249, 251 (1937).

[4]U.S. Const. art. I, Sec. 8 (3).

[5]*R.C. Tway Coal Co.* v. *Glen*, 12 F. Supp. 570, 589 (1935).

[6]Opinion of the Attorney General of Michigan, 12 RR 2d 2145, 2146 (1968).

[7]*Ibid.*, see also *Pacific Coast Dairy, Inc.* v. *Department of Agriculture of California*, 318 U.S. 285 (1943).

[8]*United States* v. *City of Chester*, 144 F.2d 415, 420 (1944).

[9]81 C.J.S. *States* Sec. 7, 871-872 (1953).

[10]47 U.S.C.A. Sec. 151 (1962).

[11]47 U.S.C.A. Sec. 153 (b) (1962).

[12]*Allen B. Dumont Laboratories, Inc.* v. *Carroll*, 184 F.2d 153, 155 (1950).

[13]*General Electric Co.* v. *Federal Radio Commission*, 31 F.(2d) 630 (app. D.C. 1929); *Federal Radio Commission* v. *Nelson Brothers*, 289 U.S. 266 (1933).

[14]*Whitehurst* v. *Grimes*, 21 F(2d) 787 (1927); see also *Federal Radio Commission* v. *Nelson Brothers*, 289 U.S. 266 (1933).

[15]Opinion of the Attorney General of Michigan, 12 RR 2d 2145, 2148 (1968); The leading case usually cited to support the contention that the field has been entirely preempted by federal law is Dumont v. Carroll (see note 12). However, other courts have noted that the Dumont decision was a narrow one and must be read in light of the particular question that was before it; i.e., a question of attempted state censorship. See Mosey Cafe, Inc. v. Licensing Board For the City of Boston, 154 N.E. 2d 585, 590 (Mass. 1958); California Democratic Council v. Arnebergh, 5 RR 2d 2073, 2074 (Cal. App. 1965).

[16]Head v. New Mexico Board of Examiners in Optometry, 374 U.S. 424 (1963).

[17]Ibid., pp. 424-425.

[18]Ibid., pp. 427-429.

[19]Ibid., pp. 429-430.

[20]Ibid., p. 432.

[21]Ibid., pp. 442-443.

[22]Ibid., p. 443.

[23]Ibid., pp. 444-446.

[24]California Democratic Council v. Arnebergh, 5 RR 2d 2073 (Cal. App. 1965).

[25]McCaw v. Fase, 216 F.2d 700 (CA 9th, 1954).

[26]McGoldrick v. Berwind-White Coal Mining Co., 309 U.S. 33, 46-47 (1940).

[27]Tri-City Broadcasting Co. v. Bowers, 158 N.E. 2d 203 (1959).

[28]Opinion of the Attorney General of Louisiana, 14 RR 2050 (1956).

[29]Opinion of the Attorney General of Missouri, 21 RR 2d 2114, 2118 (1971).

CHAPTER II

METHOD

Since this dissertation deals with statutory laws of the fifty states, the sources of my data were the official compilations of all state laws. The specific compilation used for each state is given in Table 1 at the end of the dissertation. These compilations are considered primary sources since they are prima facie the law in each state.

To ascertain what laws each state has on broadcasting, I examined all entries listed in each state's general indices under three different headings, "Broadcasting," "Radio," and "Television." Further, I checked all entries listed under these same three headings in the indices to the cumulative annual pocket supplements that accompany the general indices. In addition to checking these supplements for laws not contained in the general indices, these supplements were also examined for revisions in the law, repealed statutes and sections, and for amendments to statutes and sections. I departed from this procedure only when there was no entry for educational broadcasting under the "Broadcasting," "Radio," and "Television" headings. When this occurred, I checked each general index and its accompanying supplement under the heading "Education." This initial search of state laws was checked by repeating the entire process. The state laws covered in this dissertation were in force as of April 10, 1972.

Since I wanted a further check on the accuracy of my search of the legal literature, I corresponded with the Attorney General in each state. In a letter to each I explained that I needed to know what laws his state had on broadcasting as part of the data for my dissertation. I requested each Attorney General's assistance in sending references to those laws that in any way regulated commercial and educational radio and television broadcasting stations.

Letters were sent to the fifty Attorneys General on January 31, 1972. I received forty responses. Of these forty, thirty-one responses were helpful in that they contained references to statutes, copies of the indices to the statutes, or copies of the statutes themselves.

After examining all the statutes a second time, I checked my results against the information in these thirty-one responses. The accuracy of my search was substantiated to the extent that only three states (Iowa, Nevada, and South Dakota) sent references (one from each state) that my search had not uncovered. However, the

Nevada and South Dakota references are to laws recently passed by their current legislatures, and obviously could not have been indexed at the time I conducted my search. The Iowa reference is to a law listed under a heading other than those I discussed earlier.

The focus of this dissertation is upon only those statutes that directly affect commercial and educational radio and television broadcasting. It does not deal with statutes which regulate areas which are, at most, tangential to the operation of a broadcasting station. The excluded statutes include those on community antenna television systems (CATV), booster or translator broadcasting systems, subscription television, closed-circuit telecasts, amateur or shortwave radio stations, police radio stations, civil defense radio, and with statutory provisions applicable to public utilities generally. Neither does this study concern statutes on the manufacturing, selling, or repairing of radio and television _sets_.

All indexed entries were systematically recorded and the applicable statutes read and examined to determine whether they were relevant to the focus of the study. Those that were relevant were examined as a group and a classification system was devised. The classification system developed from the fact that the statutes show there are four major areas of regulation with which these state laws are concerned.

The first area covered by these statutes is the relationship between broadcasting and individual rights. Statutes in this area cover defamation, libel, and slander, privileged sources of information, Canon 35, juvenile hearings, eavesdropping, and public meetings. These statutes are discussed in Chapter III.

A second area covered by these state statutes is educational broadcasting and all related topics. The statutes which are relevant to this area are discussed in Chapter IV.

The third area is advertising and related matters. It includes statutes on fraudulent advertising, deceptive trade and consumer fraud practices, advertising of foods, drugs, and cosmetics, insurance, real estate, loans, professional occupations, and political advertising. Various miscellaneous topics covered by statutory law are also included in this advertising area, such as securities, liquor, bingo, cemetery lots, and apples. Statutes relevant to this advertising area are discussed in Chapter V.

The fourth area includes state statutes that affect business aspects of broadcasting. Taxes, employment practices, wages, and producers' insurance are some of the topics covered by statutory law in this area. Chapter VI covers these statutes.

Following the initial classification procedure, the statutes were further divided within each of the four major areas into groups of statutory laws that regulate the same topic. For example, in the chapter on advertising, statutes on foods, drugs, and cosmetics comprise one group, statutes on political advertising another, while statutes on fraudulent advertising, professional occupations, real estate, etc., comprise still other separate and distinct groups.

Comparative examinations were then made of the related statutes from the different states comprising each group. These examinations focused upon the following: 1) uniformity in wording across states; 2) similarities/differences/inconsistencies in purpose or intent of the law; 3) unique or noteworthy statutory provisions; and 4) enactment dates. These examinations revealed patterns among the state statutes which in turn led to analyses of related federal legislation, relevant court decisions, and administrative-agency promulgations. Further examinations and analyses of the statutes were made in accordance with the questions detailed in Chapter I.

Citations of the state statutes observe the official and preferred forms listed in <u>State Statutory Codifications</u>,[1] while other forms of citation and abbreviations generally follow <u>A Uniform System of Citation</u>.[2]

FOOTNOTES

[1] *State Statutory Codifications* (Cambridge: The Harvard Law Review Association, 1971).

[2] *A Uniform System of Citation*, Eleventh Edition (Cambridge: The Harvard Law Review Association, 1967).

CHAPTER III

BROADCASTING AND INDIVIDUAL RIGHTS

Laws of defamation have a long history dating to local courts in the middle ages and, before the Norman Conquest in 1066, to ecclesiastical tribunals.[1] There have been many catalysts that have brought changes in defamation law through the centuries, not the least of which have been the mass media. As each new medium grew into a means of mass communication, it created new problems for the courts in handling cases dealing with libel and slander. Thus, each new medium contributed in its own way to modifications and developments in defamation law to accomodate the idiosyncracies inherent in that medium. Defamation by broadcast is but the newest chapter in the history of defamation law.

Broadcast libel has been a concern of both federal and state regulatory activity. State laws on broadcast libel are almost totally uniform in their language, and yet it appears that there is no single state nor group of states that consistently acted before all the other states. However, one clear pattern does emerge from examination of the statutes. In the area concerning defamatory statements broadcast by candidates for public office, and to a lesser extent in the area of defamatory statements broadcast by persons other than the owner or licensee of a station, states' actions were prompted by judicial decisions at the federal level. Consequently, the interaction between federal and state legislation in this area will be discussed fully in this chapter.

State statutes discussed in this chapter cover three major categories: 1) Defamation/Libel/Slander, 2) The Right Of Privacy, and 3) The Right To Know. Each major category is further subdivided into those specific topics that are covered by different statutory laws. Since Defamation/Libel/Slander is the most detailed and comprehensive of the three, it receives the most discussion in this chapter. All state statutes on broadcasting and individual rights are listed in Table 2 at the end of the dissertation.

Defamation/Libel/Slander

This category contains six different topics covered by state statutes: 1) defamatory statements made by political candidates; 2) defamatory statements made by persons who are neither candidates nor licensees of stations; 3) the Uniform Single Publication Act; 4) fair reports of governmental proceedings; 5) the furnishing of libelous statements to broadcasting stations; and 6) miscellaneous.

Defamatory Statements Made By Political Candidates

Thirty-one states have made the legislative determination to immunize the owner, licensee, or operator of a broadcasting station from liability for any damages for any defamatory statement made over his broadcast facilities by candidates for public office.

Though statutes in these thirty-one states are nearly uniform in their wording, they do differ with respect to certain specifications concerning licensee liability. Fourteen states specify that the broadcast licensee is not liable for defamatory statements made "by or on behalf of any candidate for public office."[2] The specification in seven states is "by any candidate."[3] Four states specify "by a candidate"[4] and four states specify "by any legally qualified candidate."[5] Two states specify "by, on behalf of, or against any candidate."[6] However, these state statutes--although still in force at the time this study was conducted--have been superseded by a 1959 U.S. Supreme Court decision in the case Farmers Educational & Cooperative Union v. WDAY.[7] In Farmers Union, the Court held that the Communications Act of 1934 displaced the state law of defamation insofar as that law directly conflicted with the "equal opportunities" provision of Section 315. This U.S. Supreme Court decision thus settled the question whether broadcasters may be held liable for defamatory statements made by candidates for public office, saying that broadcasters are exempt from such liability.

Since the development of Farmers Union provides an insightful look at the interaction of federal and state legislation in the same area, particularly when individual rights are left unprotected, a brief historical analysis of the case is in order here.

The beginnings of Farmers Union reach back to 1932 when the Nebraska Supreme Court held in Sorensen v. Wood[8] that a broadcasting station was liable for defamatory statements uttered by a political speaker, notwithstanding the statutory provisions of Section 315 of the Communications Act which prohibits censorship of material broadcast under that section.[9] Thus, broadcasters were faced with a dilemma, i.e., they either faced prosecution for violating a federal statute prohibiting censorship, or of being liable for defamation.

The Sorensen rule went virtually unchallenged for sixteen years,[10] until 1948 when the Federal Communications Commission attempted a solution of the broadcasters' dilemma in their Port Huron decision.[11]

> In Port Huron, the issue was squarely presented: whether the provision of Section 315 denying the licensee the right to censor the 'material' of a political broadcast prohibits the station from censoring speeches broadcast by candidates which the licensee might reasonably believe to be libelous.[12]

In rejecting the interpretation of Section 315 by the Sorensen court, the FCC relied, in part, on the legislative history of Section 315. As originally proposed, Section 18 of the Radio Act of 1927 (which, when repealed, was incorporated without change into Section 315 of the Communications Act of 1934) contained both the existing prohibition against censorship as well as a provision that a broadcast licensee "shall not be liable to criminal or civil action by reason of any uncensored utterances thus broadcast."[13] However, by the time the bill became law, the provision for liability exemption was eliminated while the provision prohibiting any censorship remained intact.

After acknowledging the fact that Congress had failed to remedy the broadcasters' dilemma, the FCC went on to reaffirm in Port Huron that the prohibition of Section 315 is absolute, and no exception can be given in cases where libelous material involves the station in an action for damages. In addition, the FCC went on to read the provisions of Section 315 as relieving broadcasters of responsibility for libelous matter broadcast under the provisions of that section.[14]

However, the Federal Communications Commission was ruling on a matter of constitutional law, "that the Supremacy Clause requires that the existence of the Communications Act of 1934 oust [sic] the States of jurisdiction to impose libel laws upon broadcasts made under the provisions of Section 315."[15] Such a ruling is not within the province of administrative agencies. Thus, in attempting to remedy a dilemma caused by Congress' failure to immunize licensees, the FCC felt constrained to act in an area of law not within its jurisdiction. The FCC should have left this question to Congress and the courts.[16]

The Port Huron decision intensified the dilemma for broadcasters. If they observed the Port Huron doctrine, they might face civil and criminal defamation actions in state courts; or if they censored defamatory remarks, they would jeopardize their licenses which conceivably could be revoked by the FCC.[17] Consequently, the Port Huron doctrine met condemnation from several quarters including the broadcasting industry, Congress, the judiciary, and legal commentators.[18]

Such vigorous condemnation foreshadowed U.S. Supreme Court intervention in Farmers Union. This case arose as a result of a speech made over WDAY, Fargo, by a legally qualified candidate in the 1956 U.S. senatorial race in North Dakota. Since the station felt compelled to observe the provisions of Section 315, WDAY permitted the speech to be broadcast uncensored,[19] although the station management later admitted in their brief that they were aware the speech was defamatory.[20]

Farmers Union, accused in that speech of conspiring to establish a Communist Farmers Union Soviet in North

Dakota, sued the broadcasting station and the speaker as joint publishers. A North Dakota District Court dismissed the suit against WDAY, on the ground that Section 315 rendered the broadcasting station immune from liability. The Supreme Court of North Dakota affirmed.[21] In holding that state libel laws could not apply to WDAY, the North Dakota Supreme Court said:

> Section 315 imposes a mandatory duty upon broadcasting stations to permit all candidates for the same office to use their facilities if they have permitted one candidate to use them. Since power of censorship of political broadcasts is prohibited it must follow as a corollary that the mandate prohibiting censorship includes the privilege of immunity from liability for defamatory statements made by the speakers.[22]

The U.S. Supreme Court affirmed 5-4 in its 1959 Farmers Union decision and in so doing granted federal immunity to broadcasters from liability for libelous statements contained in speeches broadcast by legally qualified candidates for public office.[23]

Two questions emerge from the historical development of Farmers Union: 1) Why did the Sorensen rule remain unchallenged for nearly two decades? 2) Where do state laws on broadcast defamation fit into this development?

One reason for the many years of failure by broadcast licensees to challenge Sorensen is what one author calls the "docility of most licensees to regulation."[24] A remarkable example of such docility is the fact that during the nine years (1940-1949) in which the Mayflower

Doctrine[25] was enforced, no broadcaster risked his license to challenge Mayflower's no-editorializing policy.[26] It was not until the FCC issued its Editorializing By Broadcast Licensees[27] decision (which established the famous "Fairness Doctrine") that Mayflower became history.

The evidence clearly shows that broadcasters are not willing to disturb the status quo. Perhaps their docility may be accounted for by the expense of judicial review, fear of losing their licenses, or the fact that regulation has virtually never had any adverse effect on a station's income.[28] Whatever the reason, broadcasters have been especially unwilling to go to court to test defamation laws. Since broadcasters were not willing to challenge Sorensen, and since the legislative history of defamation laws shows that no legal question can be finally determined except by litigation,[29] broadcasters themselves may be held partially to blame for the FCC's controversial Port Huron decision. Since this federal decision (Port Huron) offered no concrete solutions, the states undertook to resolve the liability dilemma for broadcasters.

Inspection of the states' statutory laws on liability for defamatory political statements which are broadcast, reveals that twenty-six of the thirty-one states with such statutes enacted them after Port Huron, between the years 1949-1959.[30] It is apparent that the states recognized the ambiguous and faulty ruling on the part of the FCC, and chose to exercise their police power in matters of law not wholly precluded by federal statute or decision.

It is not really surprising, therefore, that the states decided to act, especially those states which adopted their statutes between the _Port Huron_ and _Farmers Union_ decisions. What is surprising is that New Hampshire passed its statute after _Farmers Union_; in other words, after there was really no need to do so. Equally surprising, perhaps even more so, is the fact that although _Farmers Union_ now supersedes state laws insofar as they directly conflict with the "equal opportunities" provision of Section 315, none of the thirty-one states has elected to repeal its statute. Both of these facts deserve some further comment.

New Hampshire's statute became effective on September 15, 1959, whereas _Farmers Union_ was decided June 29, 1959. As is the case with most legislatures, several months may pass between the time when a bill is introduced to the time when it becomes law. It is conceivable that the New Hampshire statute was introduced long before _Farmers Union_ was decided, or even before it was argued on March 23, 1959. The bill presumably became law after following the usual course of events dictated by legislative processes.

More interesting to note is the fact that none of the thirty-one states since 1959 has repealed its political candidate defamation statute. I believe that there are two possible explanations for this. First, as indicated in Chapter I, a state statute must be upheld unless there is found to be a conflict between the federal and state schemes of regulation, such that both cannot stand in the same area, or if there is evidence of a congressional design to preempt the field.[31] Since neither of these two situations exist, the states may see no need to repeal the applicable statutes. In addition, legislative inertia may account for some states' failure to repeal. It is not unheard of that outdated and peculiar laws are still in force in some states.

Another explanation is suggested by the fact that Farmers Union was decided by a divided court, 5-4. Had the case swung the other way, state libel laws would have been upheld. Perhaps the states are willing to let stand those laws which might become necessary should the U.S. Supreme Court reverse itself in the future.

Defamatory Statements Made By Persons Who Are Neither Candidates Nor Licensees Of Stations

This topic deals with defamatory statements made on the air by persons who are neither candidates for public office nor licensees or owners of broadcasting stations. Twenty-six states[32] have enacted statutes that immunize the owner, licensee, or operator of a broadcasting station from liability for any damages for any defamatory statement made over his facilities "by one other than such owner, licensee, or operator." However, the immunity is relinquished if it is proved by the complaining party that such owner, licensee, or operator "failed to exercise due care to prevent" the utterance of the defamatory statement. Only two of these twenty-six states, Mississippi[33] and North Dakota,[34] do not contain this qualifying provision of "failed to exercise due care."

The wording of these non-owner immunity laws is remarkably uniform from state to state. No clear pattern of legislative enactment was discerned except that Iowa passed its statute in 1939,[35] whereas twenty-two states enacted theirs between the years 1949 and 1959.[36] This was the same period during which most of these states were passing their political candidate defamation laws.

The Uniform Single Publication Act

Another kind of statute which limits a broadcasting station's liability for defamatory statements stipulates that no person shall have more than one cause of action for damages for libel founded upon any one broadcast over radio or television, and that recovery in any action shall include all damages suffered by the plaintiff (the person or organization who initiates a legal action) in all jurisdictions. This means that one cannot bring ten suits in ten courts simply because the libelous statement was broadcast by ten stations in ten cities.

Seven states have adopted this law which is cited as the Uniform Single Publication Act. This Act was adopted in 1953 by Arizona,[37] Idaho,[38] North Dakota,[39] and Pennsylvania;[40] in 1955 by California[41] and New Mexico;[42] and in 1959 by Illinois.[43] Although Arizona, California, and New Mexico are contiguous states in the Far West, the enactment of this uniform statute does not appear to be indigenous to any particular region of the United States.

Fair Reports Of Governmental Proceedings

Montana[44] and Utah[45] grant immunity to broadcasters from liability for prosecution for a fair and true broadcast of any judicial, legislative, or other public official proceeding. However, if it is proved that the broadcast was made with malice, then the broadcaster forfeits such immunity. Further, malice is not to be implied from the mere fact of broadcast. The two statutes in Montana and Utah are nearly uniform in their wording.

The Furnishing Of Libelous Statements To Broadcasting Stations

It is a misdemeanor for any person in New Jersey to knowingly deliver to any broadcasting station any defamatory or libelous statement--as though it were a fact--concerning any person, and thereby secure the broadcasting of the statement.[46] A person who violates a similar statute in Pennsylvania may be imprisoned for up to one year or fined up to $1,000 or both.[47] It is interesting to note, however, that Pennsylvania's statute stipulates that the person delivering the defamatory matter does so "intending the same for broadcasting," and does not say anything about securing the broadcasting of same as does New Jersey's law.

Miscellaneous

In this section I will discuss several miscellaneous areas of defamation covered by state statutes.

Statutes in Florida,[48] Idaho,[49] Montana,[50] and Utah[51] give broadcasters the right to require the submission of a copy of the complete script intended to be broadcast by any person over the station prior to broadcast time. Though broadcasters have the statutory right to request a script in these four states, they are not compelled to do so. The Florida law also stipulates that, once the broadcaster has exercised his right to request a script, he is relieved from liability for any defamatory statement made by the person submitting the copy of the proposed broadcast which is not contained in the copy.[52]

California,[53] Idaho,[54] New Hampshire,[55] and Utah[56] have each enacted statutes pertaining to liability for uncontrolled network broadcasts. These statutes state that if any defamatory statement is uttered in or as part of a network broadcast, liability shall be confined to the radio or television station that originated the broadcast.

Various aspects of compensatory damages resulting from broadcast libel suits are covered by statutes in fifteen states. Statutes in Georgia,[57] Louisiana,[58] Nebraska,[59] and Wyoming[60] stipulate that only actual damages[61] may be recovered by the complaining party in any action for damages for any defamatory statement broadcast. Also, only actual damages may be recovered in Indiana,[62] Mississippi,[63] and North Carolina[64] if it appears at trial that the defamatory statement was broadcast in good faith, and that a full and fair retraction was broadcast. Similar statutes in Montana,[65] Ohio,[66] and Oklahoma[67] specify certain conditions governing the broadcast of retractions. For example, the Montana law requires that the retraction be broadcast "at the same time of day as the broadcast complained of and of at least equal duration."[68] In addition, the Montana law stipulates that the retraction be broadcast within seven days following receipt by the station management of the complaining party's written notice specifying the words or acts alleged to be defamatory.[69] Oklahoma requires all television and radio stations to record and preserve all political utterances for a period of three years.[70] These recordings are to be made available to any person instituting an action for libel or defamation. In contrast to those statutes that allow the recovery of only actual damages, statutes in Arizona,[71] Idaho,[72] Iowa,[73] Nevada,[74] and Oregon[75] contain provisions that allow the complaining party to recover more than actual damages if a retraction of the libelous statement was demanded and subsequently refused.

Massachusetts[76] and Pennsylvania[77] statutes relieve broadcasters from liability for "any defamatory matter" broadcast. A Maine law states that a broadcaster is responsible "for any libel published or uttered," unless he proves that it was broadcast "without his knowledge, consent or suspicion, and that by reasonable care and diligence he could not have prevented it."[78] A North Dakota law makes it unlawful to slander the dead by means of radio.[79]

Of the forty-four states[80] that have enacted statutes on one or more topics discussed under the Defamation/Libel/Slander category, the state of Illinois is unique with respect to its criminal defamation statutes. These statutes reject the idea of punishing communications that tend merely to injure reputation, and specifically make the gist of the crime the tendency to provoke breaches of the peace.[81]

> The utterance need not actually provoke violence or criminal acts, but it is sufficient if it tends to do so. This will be a question of ultimate fact in each case. The inclusion of this element removes from the criminal area any defamatory conduct which does not tend to incite crime even though that conduct may seriously injure reputation.[82]

One final legal question concerning the state statutes on defamation deserves mention. This is the question about whether defamation by television and radio legally constitutes "libel" or "slander." A historical analysis of these twin torts is beyond the scope of this dissertation, nor is it necessary since it has been developed elsewhere.[83] However, some brief comments are in order. The question has not been entirely resolved by the courts. This is evidenced by the fact that while some courts have held broadcast defamation to be libel, others have held it to be slander. Other courts have stipulated that such defamatory broadcasts are libel if read from a script, and slander if not. Though the recent trend has been in the direction of holding such defamatory broadcasts to be slander, defamation by television and radio is still a subject of debate.[84] Most of the state statutes discussed in this chapter which cover broadcast defamation treat defamation as libel.[85]

The Right Of Privacy

This category includes statutes on privileged sources of information, Canon 35, eavesdropping, and other laws that protect to some degree the individual's right of privacy, a right considered by many to be one of the fundamental civil liberties of our system. A great deal of legislative activity in this general area by the states has been concerned with privileged sources of information.

Privileged Sources Of Information

Courts of law have long recognized the inherent rights of individuals in certain relationships with each other, and have steadfastly held their communications to be confidential and privileged. Most of us are familiar with the relationships between lawyer and client, doctor and patient, husband and wife, confessor and penitent, and reporter and informant. Of these confidential relationships, the one between reporter and informant has recently received the most attention and examination from the public and the judiciary. For example, national attention focused on the ramifications and implications of the reporter-informant relationship as a result of the controversy between the Columbia Broadcasting System and Congress over the television program, "The Selling of the Pentagon."[86] Such attention, however, has not been limited to federal jurisdictions; there has been a fair amount of legislative activity in the field by the states.

What traditionally has been a privilege enjoyed only by the print media is now being extended to encompass confidential relationships between broadcast reporters and their informants. Six states have made the legislative determination that this extended privilege be an absolute one; i.e., no person engaged in broadcast reportorial work shall be compelled to disclose the source of any information obtained by the reporter in any legal proceeding, trial, or investigation before any court.[87] In addition, the California statute goes further to state that the broadcast reporter cannot be "adjudged in contempt for refusing to disclose the source of any information procured."[88]

Five states have qualified their statutes in this area either by court decisions or by incorporating certain provisions within the statutes themselves. A Kentucky Court of Appeals held that a newspaper reporter must disclose the identity of a person who commits a crime in his presence.[89] In Maryland, a Court of Appeals held that the statute applied only to the "source" of information, and not to the "information" itself.[90] In another case the Supreme Court of Indiana held that the right created by the statute is personal to the reporter and does not render the reporter interviewing criminal defendants at their request incompetent to voluntarily testify as to statements made to him by such defendants.[91] A broadcaster in Arkansas must forfeit the statutory privilege concerning the reporter-informant relationship if it is shown that the article was broadcast "in bad faith, with malice, and not in the interest of the public welfare."[92] Ohio broadcasters are compelled by law to maintain for six months a record of those statements of information obtained. It is interesting that the "statements" themselves are to be recorded and not the "sources" who supplied those statements.[93]

The most extreme form of qualification concerning the reporter-informant confidential relationship is found in three states: Illinois,[94] Louisiana,[95] and Rhode Island.[96] After stipulating the usual provisions of the statutory privilege, these states go on to set forth the required procedures one must observe if he wishes to apply for a "divestiture of privilege." In all three states a court order divesting the privilege must be obtained by the person seeking the information. Further inspection of these statutes reveals that they have been enacted relatively recently as compared with those statutes discussed earlier.

As stated in Chapter I, all state statutes discussed in this dissertation were in force as of April 10, 1972. However, it must be noted that on June 29, 1972, the U.S. Supreme Court handed down a decision pertaining to privileged sources of information. The issue before the Court in Branzburg v. Hayes[97] was "whether requiring newsmen to appear and testify before State or federal grand juries abridges the freedom of speech and press guaranteed by the First Amendment."[98] The Court held that it does not.

The Branzburg court was more concerned with the obligation of reporters to respond to grand jury subpoenas as other citizens do,[99] rather than with the scope of permissible interrogation conducted by a grand jury. Mr. Justice Powell emphasized this point in his concurring opinion in which he said:

> The Court does not hold that newsmen, subpoenaed to testify before a grand jury, are without constitutional rights with respect to the gathering of news or in safeguarding their sources.
>
> If a newsman believes that the grand jury investigation is not being conducted in good faith he is not without remedy. Indeed, if the newsman is called upon to give information bearing only a remote and tenous relationship to the subject of the investigation, or if he has some other reason to believe that his testimony implicates confidential source relationships without a legitimate need of law enforcement, he will have access to the Court on a motion to quash and an appropriate protective order may be entered.[100]

In noting that several states have provided newsmen with statutory privileges of varying breadth,[101] the Branzburg court stated:

> There is also merit in leaving state legislatures free, within First Amendment limits, to fashion their own standards in light of the

> conditions and problems with respect to the relations between law enforcement officials and press in their own areas. It goes without saying, of course, that we are powerless to erect any bar to state courts responding in their own way and construing their own constitutions so as to recognize a newsman's privilege, either qualified or absolute.[102]

Therefore, <u>Branzburg</u> has not ousted the states from legislating statutory privileges for newsmen. Although <u>Branzburg</u> denies newsmen constitutional immunity from appearing before grand juries at all, it apparently leaves open to the judicial and legislative branches of state governments to determine for themselves the scope of permissible interrogation once the newsman has been properly summoned to appear before a grand jury.

> The asserted claim to privilege should be judged on its facts by the striking of a proper balance between freedom of the press and the obligation of all citizens to give relevant testimony with respect to criminal conduct. The balance of these vital constitutional and societal interests on a case-by-case basis accords with the tried and traditional way of adjudicating such questions.[103]

<u>Canon 35</u>

The controversy surrounding the broadcasting of courtroom trials has and continues to be a subject for debate. It is argued on the one hand that television and radio coverage can detract from the dignity of the courtroom, psychologically affect the participants, and create public misconceptions of the legal process. On the other hand, it is argued that denial of broadcast access to trials is in essence a denial of both the right to a public trial and freedom of the press.[104] This precise issue was first squarely faced by the U.S. Supreme Court in _Estes_ v. _Texas_.[105]

The conflict between broadcasters and the courts on this matter has focused on three stages of the total proceedings. The first concerns pre-trial publicity[106] where the prevailing rule is that the media be given the widest possible latitude consonant with the orderly administration of justice, as long as the presumption of innocence is not destroyed.[107] The second stage is concerned with post-trial activities, the belief here that all the media are on equal footing and are allowed to report anything about the trial that is not within the prohibited areas of libel and slander.[108] The third stage concerns activity _during_ the trial itself. _Estes_ dealt with this third stage.

The reluctance of judges in permitting broadcast access to courtroom trials can be traced to 1937 and the Bruno Hauptmann trial. Largely as a result of sensational publicity and disruptive radio broadcasts of this trial, the American Bar Association drafted Canon 35[109] of its Canons of Judicial Ethics which expresses the ABA's opinion that the broadcasting of trials should be prohibited.[110] Canon 35 has been adopted into statutory law in several states including Alaska,[111] Delaware,[112]

Nevada,[113] New Mexico,[114] New York,[115] Pennsylvania,[116] and Wyoming.[117] Delaware's statute is typical.

> The taking of photographs in the court room during the progress of judicial proceedings or radio or television broadcasting or transmitting of judicial proceedings from the court room shall not be permitted by the court.[118]

Though Estes has restricted the use of television cameras in the courtroom, it has not permanently enjoined them. Future situations are certain to arise where the balance between a fair trial and free press will have to be maintained by the courts, and decisions about whether to broadcast will be left to the judge.[119] The New York statute appears to have been written with such future situations in mind. The New York law forbids the broadcasting from a courtroom at any time, "unless permission of the chief judge of the Court of Appeals or the presiding justice of the Appellate Division in which the courtroom is located is first obtained."[120]

Miscellaneous Topics

In this section I will discuss several miscellaneous topics covered by state statutes that protect various aspects of the individual's right of privacy.

In Illinois, witnesses are not compelled to testify in any court proceeding if any portion of their testimony is to be broadcast.[121] New York has a similar statute barring the broadcasting of testimony of witnesses if such testimony was solicited "by subpoena or other compulsory process."[122]

It is unlawful for any radio or television station to make public any proceedings of any juvenile court in New Hampshire.[123] This statute also makes it unlawful for any broadcasting station to make public--without the permission of the court--the name or address or other information that might identify any juvenile delinquent arrested.[124] Iowa,[125] Nevada,[126] and Utah[127] have enacted similar provisions governing the broadcasting of a minor's name in connection with juvenile court proceedings.

State statutes prohibiting electronic eavesdropping (wiretapping) such as those in Illinois[128] and Washington[129] are not a very recent legislative activity as one might believe. Indeed, Illinois passed its first anti-wiretapping statute in 1895, and today is one of the few states that unqualifiedly prohibits all electronic eavesdropping.[130] The reason for anti-wiretapping legislation has been, of course, to protect the privacy of the individual. U.S. Supreme Court Justice Douglas has suggested that wiretapping "is a far more serious intrusion on privacy than the general writs of assistance used in colonial days. Now all the intimacies of one's private life can be recorded. This is far worse than ransacking one's desk and closets. This is a practice that strikes as deep as an invasion of the confessional."[131] Exempted from the provisions of Illinois' anti-wiretapping statutes is any radio or television broadcast "where the public is in attendance and the conversations are overheard incidental to the main purpose for which such broadcasts are then being made."[132] Employees of radio and television stations in Washington, acting in the course of bona fide news gathering duties, have the right to record and divulge communications otherwise prohibited by Washington's anti-eavesdropping statutes, provided that "consent is expressly given or if the recording or transmitting device is readily apparent or obvious to the speakers."[133] The Washington law further states that withdrawal of consent after the communication has been made shall not prohibit the broadcasting station from divulging the communication.[134]

California law prohibits the broadcasting of hearings conducted by special commissions created by the Governor to assist the Board of Corrections in its study of the subject of crime.[135] In Massachusetts, a state statute prohibits the recording or broadcasting of names of voters not yet checked as having voted at polling places.[136]

The Florida state legislature has enacted statutes that affect the individual's right of privacy in three different areas. A 1967 statute prohibits the unauthorized publication of a person's name, portrait, photograph, or other likeness in any commercial or other advertising purpose.[137] However, the provisions of this law shall not apply to the publication of a person's name or likeness in any news broadcast or telecast "as part of any bona fide news report or presentation having a current and legitimate public interest and where such name or likeness is not used for advertising purposes."[138]

Another Florida statute, enacted in 1967 and later amended in 1971, prohibits the broadcasting of the name or identity of any unmarried person under sixteen "who commits, or is the victim of, or who is a witness to or concerning any sex offense."[139] Any person who is convicted of violating the provisions of this statute may be imprisoned in the county jail for a period not exceeding one year.[140]

A 1971 statute makes it unlawful to broadcast the names of parties to any court proceeding instituted or prosecuted under Florida's Bastardy Act.[141]

The Right To Know

This category includes statutes pertaining to the broadcasting of supplementary official notices, the broadcasting of public meetings and hearings, and other matters involved with the public's right to know.

Supplementary Broadcasts

Statutes on supplementary broadcasts provide a clear example of contiguous states effects. The Pacific Northwest states of Washington, Idaho, Montana, Oregon, and Utah all have laws that allow public officials in those states to supplement by broadcast any notice which they are required by law to publish.[142] Idaho's statute is typical.

> Any official of the state of Idaho or any of its political subdivisions who is required by law to publish any notice required by law may supplement publication thereof by radio or television broadcast or both when, in his judgment, the public interest will be served thereby.[143]

Further inspection of these statutes shows the state of Washington to be the innovator in adopting such legislation, having first enacted its statute in 1951 and later amending it in 1961.[144] Idaho[145] and Montana[146] followed in 1963, Oregon in 1967,[147] and Utah in 1971.[148]

Public Meetings

The next group of laws are of special interest because both the public's right to know and the "accountability" of state legislatures are well-served in those states which have enacted them. In its comprehensive study of the fifty state legislatures, the Citizens Conference on State Legislatures noted, "Ultimately, of course, the right to know resides with the people, who get their information and form their impressions about the legislature from the news media."[149] The study found that it is a "rare legislature" which has actively encouraged press coverage of its activities, especially by opening its doors to live coverage by the electronic media.[150]

If one accepts the point of view of the Citizens Conference, it should be heartening to know that five states have enacted legislation enabling this public right to know to be enforced by law. Maine allows broadcast coverage at "all public meetings";[151] Nebraska at "all convened meetings of governing bodies of all agencies";[152] Connecticut at "any meeting of an administrative or executive board, commission, agency, committee";[153] California at "proceedings of public administrative agencies";[154] and Indiana at "all administrative bodies . . . conducting public hearings."[155] The Nebraska statute also states that any official who violates the provisions of the statute shall be deemed guilty of a misdeameanor.[156] However, as discussed earlier under the "Fair Reports Of Governmental Proceedings" subcategory, Montana and Utah protect the broadcaster from liability for prosecution for a fair and true broadcast of public proceedings.

Miscellaneous Topics

In this section I will discuss several miscellaneous topics covered by statutory laws that affect the public's right to know.

Illinois,[157] New Jersey,[158] and North Carolina[159] have enacted statutes stipulating various registration procedures for persons and organizations engaged in influencing public opinion or legislation; in short, lobbyists. In Illinois these statutes are part of its Lobbyist Registration Act, while New Jersey codifies similar provisions under its Legislative Activities Disclosure Act. In all three states, however, a broadcasting station is exempted from compliance with the law since it is viewed as a bona fide news medium, and as such comments upon public opinion and legislation in the ordinary course of its business. The state of Tennessee has enacted similar statutes applicable to persons and organizations engaged in influencing public opinion or legislation "in behalf of or in opposition to any race or color or whose activities cause or tend to cause racial conflicts or violence."[160] As in Illinois, New Jersey, and North Carolina, these Tennessee statutes also include a provision that exempts radio and television stations.[161] Thus, the public's right to know is guaranteed to some extent by statutory law in these four states which facilitate news coverage by the electronic media.

Connecticut enacted a statute in 1955 which allows authorized members of the press and radio upon the floor of either house while such house is in session.[162] No reference is made to television personnel in this Connecticut statute. Indiana allows authorized representatives of radio and television stations to be present in the voting room during an election.[163]

The provisions set forth in a California statute barring unauthorized entry to disaster areas specifically state that the statute shall not prevent duly authorized personnel of radio or television stations from entering the closed areas.[164] However, a 1970 California court decision stated that a sheriff has a statutory duty to enforce the laws of the state and maintain public order and safety, and that such duty implicitly includes discretion to permit or not permit press and reporters to cross police lines.[165] Upon proper identification, radio reporters may be admitted to the place of execution of judgment in Oklahoma.[166]

The same statutes in the four states that protect a juvenile delinquent's identity (discussed under miscellaneous topics in The Right Of Privacy category), do not apply when the delinquent act would constitute a felony if it were the act of an adult.[167]

FOOTNOTES

[1]R. C. Donnelly, "History of Defamation," 1949 *Wisconsin Law Review* 99, 100, 103 (January 1949).

[2]Arizona, California, Connecticut, Georgia, Idaho, Maine, Michigan, Mississippi, Missouri, Nevada, New Hampshire, Ohio, Utah, and Virginia.

[3]Colorado, Hawaii, Maryland, Oklahoma, Oregon, Tennessee, and Wyoming.

[4]Arkansas, Montana, South Carolina, and Wisconsin.

[5]Kentucky, New Jersey, New York, and West Virginia.

[6]Louisiana and Nebraska.

[7]360 U.S. 525 (1959).

[8]*Sorensen* v. *Wood*, 123 Neb. 348, 243 N.W. 82 (1932), *appeal dismissed* 290 U.S. 599 (1933).

[9]The *Sorensen* court dealt with provisions concerning use of broadcasting stations by legally qualified candidates, provisions that were part of Section 18 of the Radio Act of 1927. When the Radio Act was repealed, Section 18 was incorporated without change into Section 315 of the Communications Act of 1934, which reads in part: "If any licensee shall permit any person who is a legally qualified candidate for any public office to use a broadcasting station, he shall afford equal opportunities to all other such candidates for that office in the use of such broadcasting station: *provided*, that such licensee shall have no power of censorship over the material broadcast under the provisions of this section."

[10]Although a New York lower court dealt with ramifications of Section 315 during this period, that case has never been authoritatively cited. See Note, Walter A. Goldhill, "Censorship of Political Broadcasts," 58 *Yale Law Journal* 787, 789 (April 1949).

[11]*Port Huron Broadcasting Co.*, 12 F.C.C. 1069 (1948).

[12] Daniel W. Toohey, "The Avoidance of Offense: Observations on the Matter of Broadcast Censorship," 15 _Saint Louis University Law Journal_ 48, 55 (Fall 1970).

[13] 12 F.C.C. 1069, 1073 (1948).

[14] _Ibid_., pp. 1073-1074.

[15] 360 U.S. 525, 537.

[16] Gordon R. Payne, "ADMINISTRATIVE LAW: Libel Without Liability?," 37 _The Georgetown Law Journal_ 383, 387 (March 1949).

[17] Note, Harvey L. Zuckman, "Censorship of Defamatory Political Broadcasts: The Port Huron Doctrine," 34 _New York University Law Review_ 127, 132 (January 1959).

[18] _Ibid_.

[19] 360 U.S. 525, 526.

[20] Note, "The Supreme Court, 1958 Term," 73 _Harvard Law Review_ 233, 234 (November 1959).

[21] 360 U.S. 525, 526-527.

[22] 89 N.W. 2d 102, 110 (1958).

[23] 360 U.S. 525, 526.

[24] Toohey, p. 54.

[25] _Mayflower Broadcasting Corporation_, 8 F.C.C. 333 (1940).

[26] Toohey, p. 54.

[27] _Editorializing By Broadcast Licensees_, 13 F.C.C. 1246 (1949).

[28] Toohey, p. 54.

[29] Zuckman, p. 134.

[30]Montana enacted its statute in 1939, Mont. Rev. Codes Ann. Sec. 64-205 (repl. 2d 1970); Wyoming in 1947, Wyo. Stat. Ann. Sec. 1-873 (1957); and Virginia in 1948, Va. Code Ann. Sec. 8-632.1 (repl. 1957). Precise enactment dates were not found for Arkansas, Ark. Stat. Ann. Sec. 3-1108 (Supp. 1971), nor for Colorado, Colo. Rev. Stat. Ann. Sec. 41-2-6 (1963).

[31]Florida Lime & Avocado Growers v. Paul, 373 U.S. 132, 141 (1963).

[32]See states listed under "Non-Candidates, Non-Licensees" in Table 2 at the end of the dissertation.

[33]Miss. Code Ann. Sec. 1059.5(1) (1957).

[34]N.D. Cent. Code Sec. 14-02-09 (repl. 1971).

[35]Iowa Code Ann. Sec. 659.5 (1950).

[36]Wyoming enacted its statute in 1947, Wyo. Stat. Ann. Sec. 1-872 (1957), and Virginia in 1948, Va. Code Ann. Sec. 8-632.1 (repl. 1957). No precise enactment date was found for Colorado, Colo. Rev. Stat. Ann. Sec. 41-2-6 (1963).

[37]Ariz. Rev. Stat. Ann. Sec. 12-651 (1956).

[38]Idaho Code Sec. 6-702 (Supp. 1971).

[39]N.D. Cent. Code Sec. 14-02-10 (repl. 1971).

[40]Pa. Stat. Ann. tit. 12, Sec. 2090.1 (1967).

[41]Cal. Civ. Code Sec. 3425.1 et seq. (West 1970).

[42]N.M. Stat. Ann. Sections 40-27-30 to 34 (repl. 1964).

[43]Ill. Ann. Stat. ch. 126, Sections 11-15 (Smith-Hurd 1967).

[44]Mont. Rev. Codes Ann. Sec. 94-2807 (repl. 1969).

[45]Utah Code Ann. Sec. 76-40-6 (Supp. 1971).

[46]N.J. Stat. Ann. Sec. 2A:120-1 (1969).

[47]Pa. Stat. Ann. tit. 18, Sec. 4413.1 (1963).

[48]Fla. Stat. Ann. Sec. 770.03 (1964).

[49] Idaho Code Sec. 6-707 (Supp. 1971).

[50] Mont. Rev. Codes Ann. Sec. 64-206 (repl. 2d 1970).

[51] Utah Code Ann. Sec. 45-2-6 (repl. 1970).

[52] Fla. Stat. Ann. Sec. 770.03 (1964); see also Wash. Rev. Code Ann. Sec. 19.64.010 (1961).

[53] Cal. Civ. Code Sec. 48.5(2) (West 1954).

[54] Idaho Code Sec. 6-709 (Supp. 1971).

[55] N.H. Rev. Stat. Ann. Sec. 507-A:3 (repl. 1968).

[56] Utah Code Ann. Sec. 45-2-8 (repl. 1970).

[57] Ga. Code Ann. Sec. 105-714 (1968).

[58] La. Rev. Stat. Ann. Sec. 45:1353 (1951).

[59] Neb. Rev. Stat. Sec. 86-603 (1971).

[60] Wyo. Stat. Ann. Sec. 1-874 (1957).

[61] The words "actual damages" are generally construed to include all damages that the complaining party may have suffered with respect to his character, property, business, trade, profession, or occupation, and no other damages whatever. See Ind. Ann. Stat. Sec. 2-519 (IC 34-4-14-2) (repl. 1967).

[62] Ind. Ann. Stat. Sec. 2-518 (IC 34-4-14-1) (repl. 1967).

[63] Miss. Code Ann. Sec. 1059.7(2) (Supp. 1971).

[64] N.C. Gen. Stat. Sec. 99-2 (Supp. 1971).

[65] Mont. Rev. Codes Ann. Sec. 64-207.1 (Supp. 1971).

[66] Ohio Rev. Code Ann. Sec. 2739.03 (Page 1954).

[67] Okla. Stat. Ann. tit. 12, Sec. 1447.5 (1961).

[68] Mont. Rev. Codes Ann. Sec. 64-207.1 (Supp. 1971).

[69] Ibid.

[70]Okla. Stat. Ann. tit. 12, Sec. 1447.4 (1961).

[71]Ariz. Rev. Stat. Ann. Sec. 12-653.02 (Supp. 1971).

[72]Idaho Code Sec. 6-712 (Supp. 1971).

[73]Iowa Code Ann. Sec. 659.2 (Supp. 1972).

[74]Nev. Rev. Stat. Sec. 41.336 (1969).

[75]Ore. Rev. Stat. Sec. 30.160 (1971).

[76]Mass. Gen. Laws Ann. ch. 231, Sec. 91A (1959).

[77]Pa. Stat. Ann. tit. 12, Sec. 1585 (Supp. 1971).

[78]Me. Rev. Stat. Ann. tit. 17, Sec. 2203 (1964).

[79]N.D. Cent. Code Sec. 12-28-15 (1960).

[80]No statutes were found on any of the topics discussed under the Defamation/Libel/Slander category for the following six states: Alabama, Alaska, Delaware, Kansas, Rhode Island, and Vermont.

[81]Ill. Ann. Stat. ch. 38, Sections 27-1, 27-2 (Smith-Hurd 1970).

[82]Ibid. For an interesting discussion of criminal libel and the breach-of-the-peace concept, see Harold L. Nelson and Dwight L. Teeter, Jr., Law of Mass Communications (Mineola: The Foundation Press, Inc., 1969), pp. 276-282.

[83]William L. Prosser, The Law of Torts, 4th ed. (St. Paul: West Publishing Co., 1971).

[84]Ibid., pp. 753-754.

[85]Only five states specifically mention the word "slander" in their defamation statutes. See Ariz. Rev. Stat. Ann. Sec. 12-653.01 et seq. (Supp. 1971); Nev. Rev. Stat. Sec. 41.331 et seq. (1969); N.C. Gen. Stat. Sec. 99-1 (repl. 1965); N.D. Cent. Code Sec. 12-28-15 (1960); and Ohio Rev. Code Ann. Sec. 2739.03 (Page 1954).

[86]For an excellent account of the controversy between CBS and Congress concerning "The Selling of the Pentagon," see the special issue of Educational Broadcasting Review (Winter 1971-1972) which is entirely devoted to the subject.

[87]Alabama, Arizona, California, Montana, Nevada, and Pennsylvania.

[88]Cal. Evid. Code Sec. 1070 (West Supp. 1972).

[89]Branzburg v. Pound, Ky., 461 S.W. 2d 345 (1971).

[90]State v. Sheridan, 248 Md. 320, 236 A.2d 18 (1967).

[91]Lipps v. State, 258 N.E. 2d 622 (1970).

[92]Ark. Stat. Ann. Sec. 43-917 (repl. 1964).

[93]Ohio Rev. Code Ann. Sec. 2739.04 (Page Supp. 1971).

[94]Ill. Ann. Stat. ch. 51, Sec. 111 et seq. (Smith-Hurd Supp. 1972).

[95]La. Rev. Stat. Ann. Sec. 45:1451 et seq. (Supp. 1972).

[96]R.I. Gen. Laws Ann. Sec. 9-19.1-1 et seq. (Supp. 1971).

[97]40 LW 5025 (1972).

[98]Ibid.

[99]Ibid., p. 5030.

[100]Ibid., pp. 5038-5039.

[101]Ibid., p. 5032.

[102]Ibid., p. 5037.

[103]Ibid., p. 5039.

[104]18 Vanderbilt Law Review 2050 (October 1965).

[105]381 U.S. 532 (1965).

[106]For example, the famous case of _Sheppard_ v. _Maxwell_, 384 U.S. 333 (1966); _Rideau_ v. _Louisiana_, 373 U.S. 723 (1963); _Irvin_ v. _Dowd_, 366 U.S. 717 (1961); and _Baltimore Radio Show, Inc._ v. _Maryland_, _cert. denied_, 338 U.S. 912 (1950).

[107]18 _Vanderbilt Law Review_ 2049-2050 (October 1965).

[108]_Ibid_.

[109]Of the several acts of the ABA, the adoption and promotion of Canon 35 has been the most controversial. For a discussion of some of the landmarks involved in this dispute, see Karl P. Warden, "Canon 35: Is There Room For Objectivity," 4 _Washburn Law Journal_ 211 (Spring 1965).

[110]34 _Fordham Law Review_ 329 (December 1965).

[111]_Alaska Civ. R._ 46(i) (1963).

[112]_Del. Code Ann._ Super. Cr. Rule 53 (1971).

[113]_Nev. Rev. Stat._ Sections 1.220, 178.604 (1971).

[114]_N.M. Stat. Ann._ Sections 21-1-1(90), 21-2-1(27) (repl. 1970).

[115]_N.Y. Judiciary Law, Judic. Appendix_ Rule 20.5 (McKinney Supp. 1971).

[116]_Pa. Stat. Ann._, R.C.P. (tit. 12), rule 223 (1967).

[117]_Wyo. Stat. Ann._, W.R. Cr. P., Rule 50 (1971).

[118]_Del. Code Ann._ Super. Cr. Rule 53 (1971).

[119]Lee J. Belstock, "Free Press--Fair Trial--Cameras in the Courtroom," 38 _University of Colorado Law Review_ 279 (Winter 1966).

[120]_N.Y. Judiciary Law, Judic. Appendix_ Rule 20.5 (McKinney Supp. 1971).

[121]_Ill. Ann. Stat._ ch. 51, Sec. 57 (Smith-Hurd 1966).

[122]_N.Y. Civ. Rights Law_ Sec. 52 (McKinney Supp. 1971).

[123]*N.H. Rev. Stat. Ann.* Sec. 169:27 (Supp. 1971).

[124]*Ibid.*

[125]*Iowa Code Ann.* Sec. 232.27 (1969).

[126]In Nevada, these provisions are contained in Senate Bill NO. 365, approved by the Nevada assembly on March 30, 1971.

[127]*Utah Code Ann.* Sec. 55-10-94 (Supp. 1971).

[128]*Ill. Ann. Stat.* ch. 38, Sec. 14-1 et seq. (Smith-Hurd 1972).

[129]*Wash. Rev. Code Ann.* Sec. 9.73.030 et seq. (Supp. 1971).

[130]See "Committee Comments--1961," *Ill. Ann. Stat.* ch. 38, Sec. 14-1 et seq. (Smith-Hurd 1972).

[131]*Ibid.*

[132]*Ill. Ann. Stat.* ch. 38, Sec. 14-3 (Smith-Hurd 1972).

[133]*Wash. Rev. Code Ann.* Sec. 9.73.030 (Supp. 1971).

[134]*Ibid.*

[135]*Cal. Penal Code* Sec. 6028.1 (West 1970).

[136]*Mass. Gen. Laws Ann.* ch. 54, Sec. 76 (Supp. 1972).

[137]*Fla. Stat. Ann.* Sec. 540.08 (Supp. 1972).

[138]*Ibid.*

[139]*Fla. Stat. Ann.* Sec. 801.221 (Supp. 1972).

[140]*Ibid.*

[141]*Fla. Stat. Ann.* Sec. 742.09 (Supp. 1972).

[142]Delaware and Kentucky have similar statutes. See *Del. Code Ann.* tit. 6, Sec. 3801 et seq. (Supp. 1970); *Ky. Rev. Stat. Ann.* Sec. 424.195 (Baldwin's Supp. 1971).

[143]*Idaho Code* Sec. 60-110 (Supp. 1971).

[144]*Wash. Rev. Code Ann.* Sec. 65.16.130 (1966).

[145]*Idaho Code* Sec. 60-110 (Supp. 1971).

[146]*Mont. Rev. Codes Ann.* Sec. 19-201 (repl. 1967).

[147]*Ore. Rev. Stat.* Sec. 193.320 (1971).

[148]*Utah Code Ann.* Sec. 45-1-4 (Supp. 1971).

[149]John Burns, *The Sometime Governments: A Critical Study of the 50 American Legislatures* (New York: Bantam Books, Inc., 1971), p. 94.

[150]*Ibid.*, p. 95.

[151]*Me. Rev. Stat. Ann.* tit. 1, Sec. 403 (Supp. 1972).

[152]*Neb. Rev. Stat.* Sec. 84-1401 (1971).

[153]*Conn. Gen. Stat. Ann.* Sec. 1-21a (1969).

[154]*Cal. Gov't Code* Sec. 6090 (West 1966).

[155]*Ind. Ann. Stat.* Sec. 57-608 (IC 4-22-3-2) (repl. 1961).

[156]*Neb. Rev. Stat.* Sec. 84-1404 (1971).

[157]*Ill. Ann. Stat.* ch. 63, Sec. 171 et seq. (Smith-Hurd Supp. 1972).

[158]*N.J. Stat. Ann.* Sec. 52:13C-1 et seq. (1970).

[159]*N.C. Gen. Stat.* Sec. 120-48 et seq. (repl. 1964).

[160]*Tenn. Code Ann.* Sec. 39-5001 (Supp. 1971).

[161]*Ibid.*, Sec. 39-5007.

[162]*Conn. Gen. Stat. Ann.* Sec. 2-51 (1969).

[163]*Ind. Ann. Stat.* Sec. 29-5024 (IC 3-1-23-24) (Supp. 1971).

[164]*Cal. Penal Code* Sec. 409.5 (West 1970).

[165]*Los Angeles Free Press, Inc. v. City of Los Angeles*, 88 Cal. Rptr. 605, 9 C.A.3d 448 (1970).

[166] Okla. Stat. Ann. tit. 22, Sec. 1015 (1958).

[167] Iowa Code Ann. Sec. 232.27 (1969); Nevada Senate Bill NO. 365 (approved March 1971); N.H. Rev. Stat. Ann. Sec. 169:27 (Supp. 1971); and Utah Code Ann. Sec. 55-10-94 (Supp. 1971).

CHAPTER IV

EDUCATIONAL BROADCASTING

State statutes on educational broadcasting exhibit one clear pattern; it is that state legislative activity in the field generally follows the lead of federal legislation. For example, in 1952 the Federal Communications Commission issued its "Sixth Report and Order" which reserved certain VHF and UHF channel assignments for exclusive use by noncommercial television stations.[1] In the next nine years, eight states enacted laws that placed the control of educational broadcasting either under an existing state agency,[2] a specially created commission,[3] or a joint committee.[4]

Another group of states[5] enacted statutes on educational broadcasting following the passage by Congress in 1962 of the "ETV Facilities Act."[6] The purpose of this Act is to assist (through matching grants) in the construction of noncommercial educational broadcasting facilities.[7]

By far the greatest amount of legislative activity by states on educational broadcasting has occurred since Congress passed the "Public Broadcasting Act of 1967." In addition to providing for the establishment of the nonprofit "Corporation for Public Broadcasting,"[8] the 1967 Act extends the provisions of the 1962 ETV Facilities Act by making available additional appropriated funds to organizations within the states for the purpose of providing educational broadcasting to their citizenry.[9] As a result of the 1967 Public Broadcasting Act, several states have enacted statutes on educational broadcasting for the first time,[10] while others have amended or updated earlier laws.[11] Thus it appears clear that federal and Congressional action has acted as a catalyst for state regulatory activity in the field of educational broadcasting.

From the foregoing discussion one might assume that a chronological view would provide the most fruitful method of examining state laws on educational broadcasting. However, I believe that a chronological view would not facilitate analysis of the statutes by answering any of the major questions set forth in Chapter I. Therefore, factors other than chronology will be considered in the analysis of the statutes.

One of these factors is whether an existing state agency or a specially created one is given control of the development of educational broadcasting within the state. Several states have placed such development in the hands of state departments of education,[12] or universities,[13] while other states have created special educational broadcasting commissions.[14] Another factor is the relative amount of control that state legislatures give to these agencies as evidenced by the delegated powers set forth in the statutes. Some agencies are given merely an advisory role,[15] others primarily coordinating,[16] while still others are given a broad legal mandate to supervise and control all aspects of educational broadcasting within the state.[17]

State statutes discussed in this chapter are divided into two main groups. One group consists of those statutes that affect existing state agencies which control educational broadcasting; the other group of statutes affect specially created commissions. Attention will also be given to legislation dealing with local controls of educational broadcasting, advisory committees, programming, purposes and powers, and instructional television. The last part of this chapter will cover the statutory restrictions that some states have imposed on educational broadcasters. I will also discuss certain restrictions set forth in the Public Broadcasting Act of 1967 and their apparent conflict with other statutory provisions in the Communications Act of 1934. This conflict raises some intriguing questions as to the constitutionality of some laws that affect educational broadcasters.

One important point should be noted by the reader. The state statutes governing the control of educational broadcasting are quite disparate in several respects, including wording, purpose, and length. Although some may be grouped for purposes of discussion, the assumption should not be made that statutes within a group are uniform in all respects. For example, a factor may be common to a group even though it is stated differently in each statute.

All of the state statutes on educational broadcasting are cited in Table 3 at the end of the dissertation.

Specially Created Commissions

The largest group of states having similar statutes in the field is comprised of twenty-three states that have created special agencies to deal with educational broadcasting. In eleven states the agencies are called "commissions,"[18] while six states have "authorities."[19] Two states have "councils,"[20] and two states have "boards."[21] Utah created a "Joint Committee on Publicly Owned Educational Television,"[22] and educational broadcasting in South Dakota is controlled by the "State Board of Directors for Educational Television."[23] For purposes of discussion, all of these various bodies will hereafter be referred to as "commissions."

The size of these commissions ranges from five in Alabama[24] and Nevada[25] to twenty-two in Pennsylvania.[26] The terms of office (following traditional staggered terms of initial appointments) vary from three years in Iowa[27] and Massachusetts[28] to ten years in Alabama,[29] while members in South Dakota serve "at the pleasure of the Governor."[30] Members in eight states serve four-year terms.[31]

The only consistency across states concerning the make-up of the commissions is that in every state except Utah[32] the governor appoints some members to the commission, with all members governor-appointed in eight states.[33] Most states specify certain educators, legislators, cabinet members, public officials, television station representatives, and citizens who may serve as commission members. The purposes and powers of the various commissions are extremely diverse.

Advisory committees on various educational and technical television matters are found in nine of these twenty-three states,[34] and the state department of education is responsible in most cases for the coordination of in-school curricula and educational television.[35]

Since these twenty-three commissions vary considerably in many respects, few contiguous states effects are evident. However, the South Dakota laws followed similar Nebraska statutes by two years.[36] More interesting is the fact that the wording of some provisions in the New Jersey and Pennsylvania state statutes parallels the wording in the federal Public Broadcasting Act of 1967.[37] Another note of interest is that Alabama and Oklahoma, states not usually known to be in the vanguard of educational innovations, are clearly in the forefront of educational broadcasting legislation. Alabama created its commission in 1953,[38] while Oklahoma's statutes are probably the most comprehensive of all the states, and undoubtedly could serve as model legislation in the field.[39]

There are a few inconsistencies among the states on educational broadcasting legislation. An Iowa statute that expressly permits public office holders to be members of its commission[40] is in contrast to laws in Alabama,[41] Arkansas,[42] and Louisiana[43] that specifically prohibit this situation. North Dakota's statute that prohibits its commission's licensing or operation of educational broadcasting stations, as well as prohibiting the use of state funds for operation of stations,[44] stands in contrast to several other states whose laws permit these functions.[45] New Jersey statutes prohibit the issuance of bonds by its commission,[46] while Oklahoma's statutes empower the Oklahoma Educational Television Authority to issue revenue bonds to help pay the cost of educational broadcasting.[47]

Since the purposes and powers which these twenty-three states granted to their commissions vary so widely, I will further divide this group into three categories: 1) take-over commissions, which are responsible for the establishment and control of educational broadcasting within the state; 2) coordinating commissions, which act as coordinators between existing educational broadcasting facilities and those facilities set up by the commissions; and 3) advisory commissions, whose primary powers are to assess needs for educational broadcasting and make recommendations to the state legislatures. Table 3 at the end of the text lists the states in each of these three categories.

Take-Over Commissions

The first category consists of fifteen states in which the commissions are given broad supervisory powers over educational broadcasting within each state.[48] Words such as "establish," "own," "construct," "initiate," "operate," and "assume responsibility for" are found in the delegated purposes and powers of these commissions. Since New Jersey's statutory provisions are representative of the kinds of provisions found in the laws governing the commissions in these fifteen states, they will be discussed in detail.

The New Jersey Public Broadcasting Authority Act of 1968 sets forth definitions of "Authority," "Commission," "Public broadcasting," and "Public broadcasting telecommunications."[49] The definition of "Public broadcasting" includes "all aspects of noncommercial radio and television, open and closed circuit, including the production and dissemination of public and community affairs, educational, cultural and instructional information to the public at large within the State."[50] The 1968 Act establishes the New Jersey Public Broadcasting Authority,[51] whose head shall be the New Jersey Public Broadcasting Commission.[52] This commission shall have fifteen members, five ex-officio members (the Commissioner of Education, the Chancellor of Higher Education, the Commissioner of Community Affairs, the Attorney General, the State Treasurer) and ten residents of the state to be appointed by the Governor with the advice and consent of the Senate.[53] Following customary terms for initial appointments, members serve for five years and receive no compensation, but they may be reimbursed for expenses.[54] The commission is empowered to appoint an executive director, who shall be salaried and who shall serve at the will of the commission.[55]

The powers of the Public Broadcasting Authority are quite detailed; only a few of the more important ones are listed here. The authority has the power to:

> Establish, own, and operate noncommercial educational television or radio broadcasting stations, one or more public broadcasting and public broadcasting telecommunications networks or systems, and interconnection and program production facilities;
>
> Apply for, receive, and hold such authorizations and licenses and assignments and reassignments of channels from the Federal Communications Commission

> (FCC) as may be necessary to conduct its operations and prepare, and file and prosecute before the FCC all applications, reports, or other documents or requests for authorization of any type necessary or appropriate to achieve the authorized purposes of the authority;
>
> Establish State-wide equipment compatibility policies;
>
> Assume responsibility for the character, diversity, quality, and excellence of programming which is released via its licensed facilities, provided that programs or series of programs of a controversial nature shall be presented with balance, fairness and equity;
>
> Subject to the approval of the Governor, receive and administer gifts, contributions, and funds from public and private sources;
>
> Co-operate [sic] with Federal agencies, for the purpose of obtaining matching and other Federal funds;
>
> Conduct explorations, research, demonstrations, or training in matters related to public broadcasting; and
>
> Contract with program production organizations, individuals, and noncommercial educational television and radio stations within and without the State to produce, or otherwise to procure, educational television or radio programs for use by noncommercial stations within the State.[56]

In addition, the authority is to advise the Governor and Legislature on necessary appropriations; provide advisory assistance to other agencies of the State and local and regional groups regarding public broadcasting techniques, and establish and maintain a library of educational television and radio programs and related materials.[57]

The New Jersey Public Broadcasting Authority has no power to issue bonds, notes, or other obligations, or to mortgage or otherwise encumber the assets of the authority or any part of its income.[58] The Authority is also prohibited from "supporting or opposing any political party or candidate for public office, . . . and from attempting to influence the enactment of legislation."[59] New Jersey's statutes also stipulate that the activity of the Authority in the field of instructional television shall not supersede the responsibilities of the Commissioner of Education, the Chancellor of Higher Education, nor local school board governing bodies with respect to the determination of educational policies or curriculum content.[60]

The remaining fourteen states in this group have statutory provisions similar to those in New Jersey concerning delegated powers of their commissions. However, not all states concern themselves with restrictions regarding political broadcasts and/or educational policies and curriculum.

Statutes in Kentucky,[61] Maryland,[62] Massachusetts,[63] and Oklahoma[64] prohibit the broadcasting of programs advocating political candidates. Programs designed to influence legislation are prohibited by statute in Maryland,[65] Nebraska,[66] and South Dakota.[67] Educational broadcasting facilities in Nebraska,[68] Pennsylvania,[69] and South Dakota[70] may not be used for any purpose contrary to the federal Constitution or the constitution of said state.

Since the federal restriction in Section 399 of the Public Broadcasting Act of 1967 (which states, "No noncommercial educational broadcasting station . . . may support or oppose any candidate for political office")[71] applies to all educational broadcasting stations, it appears that these states want to ensure the non-political nature of educational broadcasting by placing statutory restrictions on programming at the state level. No such statutory restrictions against partisan political broadcasts are found in the statutes in Alaska, Alabama, Arkansas, Iowa, Mississippi, and Wisconsin.

In many of the statutes the wording tends to reveal the assumptions that are being made about the nature of noncommercial broadcasting (e.g., the business of "educational" versus "public" commitments), and the degree of control which the legislature is trying to maintain (e.g., by its specificity on some of these matters). It is clear from New Jersey's definition of "Public broadcasting" that noncommercial broadcasting in that state serves the entire citizenry rather than just students. In Maryland, educational programming serves both the general public and the schools. The Maryland statutes stipulate the division of responsibilities in the following manner:

> The State Board of Education shall have the sole responsibility for and control over the preparation, content, and programming of all educational television and radio programs used to supplement primary, secondary, and adult

> education curricula in the public schools of this State and shall have priority as to scheduling of television and radio programs during school hours.
>
> The Maryland Public Broadcasting Commission shall have full responsibility for and control over the preparation, content, and programming of all its programs for the general public.[72]

The Nebraska laws stipulate specific qualifications for the director of instructional television indicating a high degree of control over this area of educational broadcasting by the state legislature. The director must have a minimum of three years of successful elementary or secondary school experience and shall hold a Nebraska Administrative and Supervisory Certificate.[73] Statutes in South Carolina[74] and South Dakota[75] do not have such specific stipulations as does Nebraska; instead, general responsibilities for instructional television programming are placed under the state department of education in those states. Mississippi law places in-school programming responsibilities with the State Superintendent of Education.[76] Other states to be discussed later do not make any distinction between instructional television and public television, nor do their statutes place the responsibility for in-school programming under any particular state agency or person. Rather, these statutes generally refer to the term "educational" television with no clear definition of precisely what is meant by the term.

Some states in this category of take-over commissions have other noteworthy provisions in their statutes.

Oklahoma has a comprehensive list of the meanings of terms used in its laws, as well as detailed provisions concerning commission powers.[77] As noted earlier, a praiseworthy power of the Oklahoma commission is its authority to issue revenue bonds for the purpose of paying educational broadcasting costs.[78] The specifics of the sale and issuance of the revenue bonds are included in the statute. Another example of the power delegated to the Oklahoma Educational Television Authority is evident in the following statute.

> All counties, cities, towns, municipalities and school districts of the state and all state boards, commissions, officials, and other public agencies, notwithstanding any contrary provision of law, are hereby authorized and empowered:
>
> To lease, lend, grant or convey to the Authority at its request upon such terms and conditions as the proper authorities of such counties, cities, towns, municipalities, school districts of the state, and all state boards, commissions, officials and other public agencies may deem reasonable and fair and without the necessity for any advertisement, order of court or other action or formality other than the regular and formal action of the authorities concerned, any personal property, real property and other things of value which may be necessary or convenient to the effectuation of the authorized purposes of the Authority, including real property already devoted to public use.[79]

Another Oklahoma statute establishes a system of televised instruction that is primarily designed for persons living in industrial communities remote from campuses of colleges and universities. It authorizes the expenditure of up to one million dollars for the purpose of planning and installing the televised instruction system.[80]

Iowa,[81] Massachusetts,[82] and Pennsylvania[83] have statutory provisions allowing school boards to arrange for local operations of educational broadcasting facilities. These enabling statutes have been amended to add a state commission. This sequence of local control followed by a state supervisory agency is also found in California, Florida, New York, and Virginia, all of which will be discussed later.

Kentucky is unique among states in this category in having an expressed "Declaration of Purpose" and a broad provision giving its commission "all such constitutional powers as are necessary to its accomplishment of the purpose."[84]

Another feature of some commissions is their power to appoint advisory committees to assist with the development of educational broadcasting in the state. The Iowa commission may appoint "at least" two such advisory committees: one on general operations and policy, and one on curricula and educational matters.[85] The South Carolina commission also may appoint two advisory committees: one of educators, and one of technical experts.[86] South Dakota's commission is advised by an Instructional Television Council,[87] and Alaska's commission may appoint advisory committees.[88] The Oklahoma Educational Television Authority has power to organize and select an advisory committee, not to exceed thirty-five members.[89]

Coordinating Commissions

The second category to be discussed consists of six states whose commissions for the most part act as coordinators between existing educational broadcasting facilities and those facilities set up by each commission.[90] In short, these commissions are not empowered with such broad controls as are the "take-over" commissions in the first category. Words such as "coordinate," "cooperate," "advise," and "assist" characterize the purposes and powers of these six commissions. The provisions in Virginia's statutes are typical of those found in these six states and are discussed here in detail.

Virginia's Educational Television Facilities Act of 1962 sets forth definitions of "Television station," "Nonprofit," "Council," and "Project."[91] "Council" means the Virginia Advisory Council on Educational Television, which consists of thirteen governor-appointed members who serve for four years and receive actual and necessary travel and subsistence expenses.[92] The Council is authorized to make an inventory of existing facilities for educational television, to survey the need for construction of additional facilities, and on the basis of this information, develop a program for construction and operation of public facilities which will, in conjunction with existing facilities, furnish adequate educational television programs throughout the state.[93] The Council shall also prepare a "State plan" which will include the educational television facilities program developed, and which shall provide for the establishment of television stations.[94]

Other powers of the Virginia Advisory Council on Educational Television are:

> To accept . . . any grant, gift, or contribution made to assist in meeting the cost of carrying out the purposes of this chapter [Chapter 16--Educational Television].
>
> To assist localities in planning and developing educational television facilities.
>
> To produce and distribute educational television programs to any area of the State, . . . and to acquire property and construct, maintain and operate a facility or facilities for production of educational or cultural television programs.
>
> To promulgate rules and regulations for carrying out the purposes of this chapter.[95]

The Council is also authorized to make provisions for a State educational television network interconnecting educational television stations serving Virginia.[96] Other statutes state that the governing body of any city, county, or town may provide for the establishment of educational television stations, the operation of which shall be under the direction of the school board of the establishing locale.[97] State financial assistance for educational broadcasting in Virginia is delineated in one statute which reads: "The contribution by the State to the cost of any project for educational television shall not exceed one half of the cost thereof, except for technical services."[98]

While the above statutes do not specifically state what the purpose of educational television is in the state of Virginia, this lack of definition or purpose is not unique to that state, witness states discussed in the section on take-over commissions. Other states in this section also do not concern themselves with clearly defining the purposes or nature of educational television in their statutes. For example, Nevada's definition of "educational television" is circular, defining the term to mean the "kind of programming used on educational television."[99] Ohio's definition of "educational television" is very broad and means "television programs which serve the educational needs of the community."[100] Louisiana statutes give the purpose of public television as furthering the education and cultural enrichment of its citizens.[101] West Virginia has a similar law.[102]

The Nevada statutes define "instructional television" as "educational television concerned exclusively with formal instruction,"[103] and places it under a special council.[104] The State Department of Education has sole responsibility and control over instructional television programs in Louisiana.[105]

In this group of six states having coordinating commissions, only Louisiana places any restrictions on political programming.

> No station licensed to the Authority shall be used for, nor shall any network or local programs be devoted to, the presentation of biased or one-sided aspects of partisan politics, or to advocating or opposing any present or prospective political candidacy, or to advocating or opposing any legislation currently being considered or prepared.[106]

Other interesting provisions found in these state statutes deserve mention. One is the creation of the Louisiana Corporation for French Language Television, known as "Television-Louisiane." It is empowered to establish and operate at and in conjunction with the University of Southwestern Louisiana, at Lafayette.[107] Another provision in the Louisiana statutes is the section providing for an advisory board in each congressional district of the state in which an educational television station licensed to the commission is located. The law further states that control over programming during local option time is vested in the advisory board for each station.[108]

A provision in the Ohio statutes allows county funds derived from a general tax levy to be used for support of educational television.[109] The Utah statutes seek to "discourage the proliferation of unco-ordinated" [sic] educational broadcasting facilities by providing for the establishment of a state-wide system.[110]

Advisory Commissions

This third category consists of North Dakota and Washington, states with weak educational broadcasting commissions. The North Dakota Educational Broadcasting Council was created for the purpose of "encouraging" the development of educational broadcasting in the state.[111] There is one interesting section in the North Dakota statutes. If the license of the educational radio station located at the University of North Dakota is transferred to private ownership, one of the conditions of such transfer is that "perpetual rights be retained for the use of the station for observation by the students taking courses in radio communication at the university."[112]

The state of Washington has perhaps the weakest commission among the twenty-three states in this group. The duties of the Washington State Educational Television Commission shall be to "promote the study" of educational broadcasting in the state, and to make recommendations to the superintendent of public instruction and to the legislature "during the month of November of each even-numbered year."[113]

Existing State Agencies

The second main group of states having statutory laws in the field is comprised of twelve states that have placed the control of educational broadcasting under the jurisdiction of an existing state agency. In six states this agency is the state board of education,[114] while in three states it is a university.[115] In the remaining three states, control is placed in New York's Board of Regents,[116] California's Department of General Services,[117] and Montana's Superintendent of Public Instruction.[118]

The six states in which the legislature has vested the state board of education with the supervision of educational broadcasting are Delaware, Florida, Georgia, Oregon, Rhode Island, and Tennessee. Generally, these boards of education are given broad powers to establish an educational broadcasting network in the state, and to accept federal and state funds that will enable them to carry out the statutory provisions. In Delaware, the State Board of Education took over all obligations of the former Educational Television Board.[119]

Since boards of education are in power in these six states, one might expect broadcast facilities to be used more for ITV purposes than for ETV purposes. However, only Oregon behaves in this manner. In fact, "educational television and radio" is defined by Oregon's statutes to mean:

> programs for direct teaching, programs for instructional enrichment, and programs for in-service education of teachers which are transmitted for viewing or listening in connection with instruction in public elementary and secondary education by state-operated educational television and radio stations.[120]

In contrast to Oregon, other statutory purposes such as Tennessee's "benefit of out-of-school adults,"[121] Rhode Island's "to all the citizens,"[122] and Florida's "raising living and educational standards of the citizens and residents of the state,"[123] attest to a broader sense of purpose of educational broadcasting. These same three states also provide for advisory committees to assist the state board of education in fulfilling the purpose of the law.[124]

Florida's statutes are unique among these six states because they provide for local school board ownership and operation of an educational television system. No system may be established, however, until the local board first obtains the approval of its proposed plans for operation and financial support by the department of education.[125] In addition, each educational television system must operate with an advisory committee of administrators, educators, and lay people from the district being served by the station.[126] The advisory committee acts as an intermediary between the licensee of the educational television system and the manager of the system. Some of the advisory committee's duties include making recommendations to the licensee relating to personnel, course offerings, finances, and general policies it believes to be in the best interest of the system.[127] If the licensee is a school board and if it acts adversely to such recommendations, the advisory committee may appeal the action to the state department of education.[128]

Statutory laws on educational broadcasting in California and New York have an organizational pattern similar to that of Florida. In New York the Board of Regents is empowered to "incorporate any group" for the purpose of constructing, owning, or operating a "nonprofit and noncommercial educational television station."[129] Any such corporation is subject to the general supervision and control of the Board of Regents, and must render to it an annual report upon such matters as the Regents may require.[130]

In addition to the corporations formed for the purpose of providing educational television, the law authorizes the Board of Regents to make "additional apportionments to school districts" for the purpose of encouraging such districts to install and operate broadcast or CCTV systems, or receiving equipment for the improvement of classroom instruction.[131] Any school district planning to establish such an ITV program must first submit an application to the Regents detailing the purposes of the program, procedures of operation, cost estimates, and detailed procedures to be used for evaluating the improvement of classroom instruction.[132] The Regents may also extend to the people at large increased educational opportunities and facilities, and in carrying out this provision may lease and operate a television station in New York City.[133]

In California, the Department of General Services took over functions formerly administered by the Television Advisory Committee.[134] The Department is empowered to "prepare a plan for television to serve the educational needs of the state," and to coordinate the activities of the various state agencies concerned with television for educational purposes.[135] Although the Department does not have any jurisdiction over educational content broadcast by stations,[136] it does have authority to review "all applications for television licenses" before they are submitted to the Federal Communications Commission.[137] This authority includes applications submitted for or on behalf of any school district, state college, or the University of California.[138]

The California statutes also provide for the establishment of an "Instructional Television Pilot Program."[139] This two-year program provides classes for adults by television for home reception. This pilot program was to be operative until June 30, 1972, with an evaluative report on the program's effectiveness made to the 1972 legislature by the Superintendent of Public Instruction.[140]

As the foregoing discussion of the California, Florida, and New York statutes indicates, a pattern of local control with a state supervisory agency is emerging in states with large urban centers.

Another state agency given a degree of control of educational broadcasting in some states is the state university. Only Maine, New Mexico, and Vermont have this provision in their statutes.

Vermont is the most direct in that the trustees of the University of Vermont and state agricultural college are given the mandate to provide a statewide educational television network.[141] They are to be assisted by an instructional television committee for the determination of in-school programming,[142] and by an educational television broadcasting council for consultation in carrying out the statutory purposes.[143]

The center for broadcasting and international communications at New Mexico State University may cooperate with existing ETV facilities and provide bilingual programming to serve the southern region of the state and adjoining area of Mexico.[144]

In Maine, a Committee on Maine Public Broadcasting was created and empowered to make recommendations and to advise the trustees of the University of Maine on matters pertinent to public broadcasting.[145] The University of Maine was given the power to operate and manage public broadcasting within the state, effectively reducing the Committee to an advisory position.

One state, Montana, holds a unique position among all thirty-five states that have legislation on educational broadcasting.[146] In Montana the control over educational television is not vested in a commission nor in a state agency, but rather in one individual, the Superintendent of Public Instruction.[147] He has the power to determine educational television needs of schools and universities, and to procure educational programs for their purposes.[148] The Superintendent of Public Instruction is assisted by an advisory committee (which he appoints) of educators, a television industry representative, and a "representative from the general public."[149]

Of the twelve states which place educational broadcasting under an existing state agency, only Florida,[150] New York,[151] and Rhode Island[152] specifically prohibit use of facilities for partisan political-candidate programming or influencing legislation. The Florida statute will be discussed in more detail in the next section in this chapter.

Restrictions

The last part of this chapter will deal with various statutory restrictions which some states have imposed on educational broadcasters. These restrictions give rise to redundancy and conflict between some federal and state laws on educational broadcasting. One of these conflicts raises some constitutional questions.

Federal law requires each educational FM broadcasting station[153] and each educational television station[154] to furnish a "non-profit and noncommercial broadcast service." Except for a few amended sections concerning programs produced by, at the expense of, or furnished by persons other than licensees, and the payment of line charges by someone other than licensees, federal law stipulates for educational FM stations that "no announcements promoting the sale of a product or service shall be broadcast in connection with any program."[155] The phrase "(visual or aural)" is inserted after "announcements" in the federal law affecting ETV stations.[156] Therefore, it appears that statutes in Oklahoma[157] and Rhode Island[158] that prohibit "any individual, company, corporation, or organization to advertise . . . its products or services" over the station's educational facilities are redundant.

Several states place restrictions on who may sit as members on educational broadcasting commissions. Statutes in Alabama,[159] Arkansas,[160] and Louisiana[161] state that a commission member may not hold "any other office of profit or trust under the United States, . . . or any political subdivision thereof." The Louisiana statute goes on to prohibit any members of its Educational

Television Authority from having any financial interest in any of the facilities with which the Authority is empowered to deal.[162] The Public Broadcasting Act of 1967 sets forth similar restrictions for officers of the Corporation for Public Broadcasting, and these state statutes appear to be following the federal legislation in forestalling any possible conflict of interest on the part of commission members, and thus safeguard the public's interest. The New York Board of Regents is empowered by law to terminate a corporate charter if said corporation employs a person who is a member of an organization deemed "subversive" by the Board.[163]

Restrictions pertaining to church-state separation are found in Kentucky and Massachusetts. The Kentucky Authority for Educational Television is prohibited by statute from allowing the use of its facilities by, or in aid of, any church.[164] Statutes in Massachusetts prohibit the executive committee for ETV from providing or sponsoring programs wherein "any denominational religious doctrine is inculcated, or any programs founding, maintaining or aiding any church."[165]

In Nebraska a person is designated by the Educational Television Commission to screen all programs to make certain they do not appeal to the prurient interests of the viewer.[166] A Mississippi statute prohibits educational television stations in the state from carrying any

SIECUS programming.[167] SIECUS is the acronym for "Sex Information and Education Council of U.S."[168]

Several states have restrictions on instructional television programming.[169] In most cases, the restriction requires that in-school programming must be consistent with state curricula as determined by the state board of education.

A major type of statutory programming restriction is that which deals with propaganda, subversive matter, advocacy of political candidates and parties, and attempts to influence legislation. These statutes, discussed earlier in this chapter, complement Section 399 of the Public Broadcasting Act of 1967 which states: "No noncommercial educational broadcasting station may engage in editorializing or may support or oppose any candidate for political office."[170] However, there is another facet to this relationship, for Section 398 of the Public Broadcasting Act states: "Nothing contained in sections 390-399 [sections 390-395 deal with grants for noncommercial educational broadcasting facilities; sections 396-399 cover the Corporation for Public Broadcasting] of this title [Title 47 of the U.S. Code is 'Telegraphs, Telephones, and Radio Telegraphs'] shall be deemed (1) to amend any other provision of, or requirement under this chapter" [Chapter 5 is "Wire or Radio Communication"].[171] This chapter also includes the "public interest"[172] standard which is as "binding upon noncommercial licensees as it is upon those who operate for profit."[173]

The "public interest" standard was applied successfully in a 1970 court action brought by the University of Maine against the State of Maine.[174] The case, State of Maine v. University of Maine, was concerned with the validity of a Maine statute enacted in 1963 (a verbatim copy of a 1957 Florida statute)[175] which contained the following restrictions:

> None of the facilities, plant or personnel of any educational television system which is supported in whole or in part by state funds shall be used directly or indirectly for the promotion, advertisement or advancement of any political candidate for any municipal, county, state or federal office or for the purpose of advocating or opposing any specific program, existing or proposed, of governmental action which shall include, but shall not be limited to, constitutional amendments, tax referendums or bond issues. Any person convicted of a violation of any provision of this section shall be punished by a fine of not more than $5,000 or by imprisonment for not more than 11 months, or by both.[176]

The University of Maine, licensee of educational broadcasting stations in the state, charged that this statute was in direct conflict with the Federal Communications Act of 1934 as amended.

In its judgment for the University of Maine, the Maine Supreme Court noted the following:

> In today's world nearly all important political and social issues are the subject of either 'existing or proposed' programs of 'governmental action.' Thus, obedience to the

> statute would deprive licensee's viewers of any informational programs of this nature.[177]

The Maine Supreme Court went on to say that "A state law which effectively prevents the licensee from discharging this 'public interest' obligation and thereby satisfying the license requirement cannot stand."[178] The Maine statute was declared as violating the provisions of Article VI, Cl. 2 of the U.S. Constitution, and was therefore unenforceable.[179] Subsequently, the Maine statute was repealed.[180]

By then, the Florida statute was amended to provide that:

> in the general elections of 1968 and 1970, candidates for offices appearing on a statewide ballot may be provided equal time in the general election on an experimental basis and for purposes of evaluating whether such provision of television free time to such candidates can materially reduce the excessive cost of campaigns. Provisions of such equal time shall be in accordance with reasonable rules and regulations prescribed by the state board of education or the board of regents, whichever has authority in the premises.[181]

This political experiment provided by law in Florida has not been continued, and the statute has since been amended to read:

> None of the facilities, plant, or personnel of any educational television system which is supported in whole or in part by state funds shall be used directly or indirectly for the promotion, advertisement, or advancement of any political candidate for any municipal, county, legislative, congressional, or state office. However, fair, open, and free discussion between political candidates for municipal, county, legislative, congressional, or state office may be permitted

> in order to help materially reduce the excessive cost of campaigns and to insure that the citizens of Florida shall be fully informed about such issues and candidates in such campaigns. The above provisions shall apply to the advocacy for, or opposition to any specific program, existing or proposed, of governmental action which shall include, but shall not be limited to, constitutional amendments, tax referendums, and bond issues. The provisions of this paragraph shall be in accordance with reasonable rules and regulations prescribed by the state board of education or the board of regents, whichever has authority in the premises.[182]

The reader should note the wording and development of the Florida statute from a law deemed unconstitutional in Maine, to a law now in conformity with constitutional guidelines. The Florida statute is unique among the ten states[183] discussed in this chapter that have restrictions on political candidate advocacy.

From the foregoing discussion, it appears that the restrictions on educational broadcasters vis-a-vis Section 399 of the Public Broadcasting Act are posing many difficulties for the states. For not only does Section 399 appear to be in conflict with the "public interest" standard of the Communications Act, more important, its no-editorializing provision appears to abridge the free speech provisions of the First Amendment to the U.S. Constitution. Perhaps this accounts for the states which enacted a provision that educational broadcasting facilities shall not be used for any purposes contrary to the Constitution of the United States.[184] Other states explicitly state that all rules and regulations governing educational broadcasting in their state shall be in conformity with federal laws applying to noncommercial educational broadcasting stations.[185] However, such attempts by the states only serve to reinforce the status quo, and thereby inhibit the vigorous growth and freedom of educational broadcasters in serving the public interest. These noncontentious laws are not likely to give rise to a test case which would help to resolve the inconsistency of the present law.

In Maine v. Maine, the legality of the no-editorializing provision of Section 399 was not considered by the court. In referring to Section 399, the Maine Supreme Court said: "Whether or not this provision violates First Amendment principles need not concern us here."[186]

Therefore, what could have been a test case for editorializing by educational broadcasters did not materialize and thus the provisions of Section 399 remain in force. However, as one legal commentator has pointed out, the provision prohibiting educational stations from using their facilities to support political candidates will probably receive little negative reaction, but the provision barring educational stations from editorializing is another matter.[187] Perhaps some educational broadcasters will not want to editorialize. But if an educational broadcaster wishes to serve the public interest by presenting well-researched, factual, and reasoned editorials on important public issues, he is effectively barred from doing so by Section 399.[188] However, whether the educational broadcaster will or will not editorialize is one question. The more serious question is whether the legislative ban on advocacy abridges the free speech provisions of the First Amendment to the Constitution.[189]

The current situation facing educational broadcasters is redolent of a similar one that affected commercial broadcasters during the nine years (1940-1949) in which the FCC's *Mayflower Doctrine*[190] was enforced. During that period, no broadcaster risked his license to challenge *Mayflower's* no-editorializing provision.[191] If the docility by commercial broadcasters in the face of regulation was apparent at that time, then it is not surprising that educational broadcasters are somewhat hesitant to initiate court challenges now, especially since their adversary also controls the purse strings.

It should be noted that it took nine years before the Federal Communications Commission reversed *Mayflower* in its 1949 *Editorializing By Broadcast Licensees*[192] decision, and that Section 399 only became law in 1967. Perhaps in time, Section 399 will suffer the same fate as *Mayflower*.

However, these two situations are not entirely parallel. That is, *Mayflower* was an administrative decision on the part of the FCC, and its subsequent reversal was a proper exercise of the authority granted to the Commission. In contrast, Section 399 is a law resulting from Congressional action, and as such, cannot be repealed nor its effects reversed by a ruling on the part of an administrative agency such as the Federal Communications Commission. Whether Section 399 conflicts with the "public interest" clause of the Communications Act of 1934, and more important, whether its no-editorializing provision abridges First Amendment free speech guarantees, will have to be decided by the courts. However, if no court action is forthcoming and action by Congress proves necessary, the outlook for editorializing by educational broadcasters appears very dim indeed.

FOOTNOTES

[1]"Sixth Report and Order," 17 Fed. Reg. 3905, 3908 (May 2, 1952). The "Sixth Report and Order" formally adopted recommendations contained in the FCC's "Third Notice of Further Proposed Rule Making," 16 Fed. Reg. 3072, 3079-3080 (April 7, 1951).

[2]New York, Oregon, and Rhode Island.

[3]Alabama, Arkansas, Ohio, and South Carolina.

[4]Utah.

[5]Georgia, Kentucky, Maryland, Nebraska, South Dakota, Vermont, and Virginia.

[6]47 U.S.C.A. Sec. 390 et seq. (Supp. 1972).

[7]<u>Ibid</u>., Sec. 390.

[8]<u>Ibid</u>., Sections 396-399.

[9]47 U.S.C.A. Sec. 390 et seq. (Supp. 1972).

[10]Alaska, Delaware, Iowa, Mississippi, Montana, Nevada, New Jersey, New Mexico, North Dakota, Washington, and Wisconsin.

[11]California, Florida, Louisiana, Maine, Massachusetts, Oklahoma, Pennsylvania, Tennessee, and West Virginia.

[12]See states listed under "State Boards Of Education" in Table 3 at the end of the dissertation.

[13]See states listed under "Universities" in Table 3.

[14]See states listed under "Specially Created Commissions" in Table 3.

[15]North Dakota and Washington.

[16]See states listed under "Coordinating Commissions" in Table 3.

[17]See states listed under "Take-Over Commissions" in Table 3.

[18]Alabama, Alaska, Arkansas, Maryland, Massachusetts, Nebraska, Nevada, Ohio, Pennsylvania, South Carolina, and Washington.

[19]Kentucky, Louisiana, Mississippi, New Jersey, Oklahoma, and West Virginia.

[20]North Dakota and Virginia.

[21]Iowa and Wisconsin.

[22]Utah Code Ann. Sec. 53-42-1 (repl. 1970).

[23]S.D. Compiled Laws Ann. Sec. 13-47-1 (Supp. 1971).

[24]Ala. Code tit. 52, Sec. 628 (1960).

[25]Nev. Rev. Stat. Sec. 398.100 (1971).

[26]Pa. Stat. Ann. tit. 71, Sec. 1188.2 (Supp. 1971).

[27]Iowa Code Ann. Sec. 8A.8 (Supp. 1972).

[28]Mass. Gen. Laws Ann. ch. 6, Sec. 158 (Supp. 1972).

[29]Ala. Code tit. 52, Sec. 628 (1960).

[30]S.D. Compiled Laws Ann. Sec. 13-47-1 (Supp. 1971).

[31]Kentucky, Mississippi, Nebraska, Nevada, Ohio, Virginia, Washington, and Wisconsin.

[32]Utah Code Ann. Sec. 53-42-1 (repl. 1970).

[33]Alabama, Alaska, Arkansas, Maryland, Massachusetts, Nevada, Virginia, and Washington.

[34]Alaska, Iowa, Louisiana, Nevada, Oklahoma, South Carolina, South Dakota, West Virginia, and Virginia.

[35]Louisiana, Maryland, Mississippi, Nebraska, New Jersey, South Carolina, and South Dakota.

[36]Neb. Rev. Stat. Sec. 79-2101 et seq. (1971); S.D. Compiled Laws Ann. Sections 13-47-1, 13-47-6, 13-47-18 (Supp. 1971), Sections 13-47-2 to 13-47-5, 13-47-7 to 13-47-17 (1967).

[37]Compare N.J. Stat. Ann. Sec. 48:23-7 (Supp. 1971) with Sec. 396(g) of the Public Broadcasting Act of 1967, cited as 47 U.S.C.A. Sec. 396(g) (Supp. 1972). Compare also Pa. Stat. Ann. tit. 71, Sec. 1188.1 (Supp. 1971) with Sec. 396(a) of the Public Broadcasting Act, 47 U.S.C.A. Sec. 396(a) (Supp. 1972).

[38]Ala. Code tit. 52, Sec. 627 (1960).

[39]Okla. Stat. Ann. tit. 70, Sec. 23-101 et seq. (Supp. 1971).

[40]Iowa Code Ann. Sec. 8A.10 (Supp. 1972).

[41]Ala. Code tit. 52, Sec. 628 (1960).

[42]Ark. Stat. Ann. Sec. 80-3902 (Supp. 1971).

[43]La. Rev. Stat. Ann. Sec. 17:2503 (Supp. 1972).

[44]N.D. Cent. Code Sec. 15-65-04 (repl. 1971).

[45]For example, see Alaska Stat. Sec. 14.58.070(3) (1971); La. Rev. Stat. Ann. Sec. 17:2501(C1) (Supp. 1972); Neb. Rev. Stat. Sections 79-2103(2) and 79-2105 (1971); N.J. Stat. Ann. Sec. 48:23-7 (Supp. 1971); Okla. Stat. Ann. tit. 70, Sec. 23-101 (Supp. 1971); and S.D. Compiled Laws Ann. Sec. 13-47-12 (1967).

[46]N.J. Stat. Ann. Sec. 48:23-8 (Supp. 1971).

[47]Okla. Stat. Ann. tit. 70, Sec. 23-109 (Supp. 1971).

[48]See states listed under "Take-Over Commissions" in Table 3 at the end of this dissertation.

[49]N.J. Stat. Ann. Sec. 48:23-2 (Supp. 1971).

[50]Ibid.

[51]Ibid., Sec. 48:23-3.

[52]Ibid., Sec. 48:23-4.

[53]Ibid.

[54]*Ibid.*

[55]*Ibid.*, Sec. 48:23-5.

[56]*Ibid.*, Sec. 48:23-7.

[57]*Ibid.*

[58]*Ibid.*, Sec. 48:23-8.

[59]*Ibid.*, Sec. 48:23-9.

[60]*Ibid.*, Sec. 48:23-10.

[61]*Ky. Rev. Stat. Ann.* Sec. 168.100(2) (Baldwin's Supp. 1971).

[62]*Md. Ann. Code* art. 77, Sec. 161(e) (repl. 1969).

[63]*Mass. Gen. Laws Ann.* ch. 71, Sec. 13I (1969).

[64]*Okla. Stat. Ann.* tit. 70, Sec. 23-102 (Supp. 1971).

[65]*Md. Ann. Code* art. 77, Sec. 161(e) (repl. 1969).

[66]*Neb. Rev. Stat.* Sec. 79-2103(14) (1971).

[67]*S.D. Compiled Laws Ann.* Sec. 13-47-17 (1967).

[68]*Neb. Rev. Stat.* Sec. 79-2103(14) (1971).

[69]*Pa. Stat. Ann.* tit. 71, Sec. 1188.3(4) (Supp. 1971).

[70]*S.D. Compiled Laws Ann.* Sec. 13-47-17 (1967).

[71]47 U.S.C.A. Sec. 399 (Supp. 1972).

[72]*Md. Ann. Code* art. 77, Sec. 161(c,d) (repl. 1969).

[73]*Neb. Rev. Stat.* Sec. 79-2111 (1971).

[74]*S.C. Code Ann.* Sec. 21-60.5 (Supp. 1971).

[75]*S.D. Compiled Laws Ann.* Sec. 13-47-21 (Supp. 1971).

[76]*Miss. Code Ann.* Sec. 8946-107(8) (Supp. 1971).

[77]*Okla. Stat. Ann.* tit. 70, Sections 23-104, 23-106 to 23-109 (Supp. 1971).

[78]*Ibid.*, Sec. 23-109.

[79]*Ibid.*, Sec. 23-118.

[80]*Ibid.*, Sec. 2166.

[81]*Iowa Code Ann.* Sec. 8A.19 (Supp. 1972).

[82]*Mass. Gen. Laws Ann.* ch. 71, Sec. 13F (Supp. 1972).

[83]*Pa. Stat. Ann.* tit. 24, Sec. 5-523(b) (Supp. 1971).

[84]*Ky. Rev. Stat. Ann.* Sections 168.010, 168.100 (Baldwin's Supp. 1971).

[85]*Iowa Code Ann.* Sec. 8A.13 (Supp. 1972).

[86]*S.C. Code Ann.* Sec. 21-60.1 (1962).

[87]*S.D. Compiled Laws Ann.* Sec. 13-47-21 (Supp. 1971).

[88]*Alaska Stat.* Sec. 14.58.070 (1971).

[89]*Okla. Stat. Ann.* tit. 70, Sec. 23-103 (Supp. 1971).

[90]See states listed under "Coordinating Commissions" in Table 3 at the end of this dissertation.

[91]*Va. Code Ann.* Sec. 22-332 (Supp. 1971).

[92]*Ibid.*, see also Sec. 22-335 (repl. 1969).

[93]*Ibid.*, Sec. 22-336 (repl. 1969).

[94]*Ibid.*, Sec. 22-338.

[95]*Ibid.*, Sec. 22-334 (Supp. 1971).

[96]*Ibid.*, Sec. 22-344.2.

[97]*Ibid.*, Sec. 15.1-23 (repl. 1964).

[98]*Ibid.*, Sec. 22-344 (Supp. 1971).

[99] *Nev. Rev. Stat.* Sec. 398.030 (1971).

[100] *Ohio Rev. Code Ann.* Sec. 3353.01(A) (Page Supp. 1970).

[101] *La. Rev. Stat. Ann.* Sec. 17:2501 (Supp. 1972).

[102] *W. Va. Code Ann.* Sec. 10-5-1 (repl. 1969).

[103] *Nev. Rev. Stat.* Sec. 398.060 (1971).

[104] *Ibid.*, Sec. 398.150.

[105] *La. Rev. Stat. Ann.* Sec. 17:2505 (Supp. 1972).

[106] *Ibid.*, Sec. 17:2506.

[107] *Ibid.*, Sections 25:701-703 (1969).

[108] *Ibid.*, Sec. 17:2505 (Supp. 1972).

[109] *Ohio Rev. Code Ann.* Sec. 5705.05 (Page Supp. 1971).

[110] *Utah Code Ann.* Sec. 53-42-2 (repl. 1970).

[111] *N.D. Cent. Code* Sec. 15-65-01 (repl. 1971).

[112] *Ibid.*, Sec. 15-11-27.

[113] *Wash. Rev. Code Ann.* Sec. 28A.91.060 (1970).

[114] See states listed under "State Boards Of Education" in Table 3.

[115] See states listed under "Universities" in Table 3.

[116] *N.Y. Educ. Law* Sec. 236 (McKinney 1969).

[117] *Cal. Gov't Code* Sec. 14716 (West Supp. 1972).

[118] *Mont. Rev. Codes Ann.* Sec. 75-5710 (2d repl. 1971).

[119] *Del. Code Ann.* tit. 14, Sec. 132 (Cum. Supp. 1970).

[120] *Ore. Rev. Stat.* Sec. 354.410(1) (1971).

[121] *Tenn. Code Ann.* Sec. 49-3807 (Supp. 1971).

[122] *R.I. Gen. Laws Ann.* Sec. 16-28-1 (Reenactment of 1969).

[123] *Fla. Stat. Ann.* Sec. 229.805 (Supp. 1972).

[124] *Fla. Stat. Ann.* Sec. 229.805(3b) (Supp. 1972); *R.I. Gen. Laws Ann.* Sec. 16-28-4 (Reenactment of 1969); *Tenn. Code Ann.* Sec. 49-3803 (Supp. 1971).

[125] *Fla. Stat. Ann.* Sec. 230.60 (Supp. 1972).

[126] *Ibid.*, Sec. 230.61.

[127] *Ibid.*

[128] *Ibid.*, Sec. 230.61(5).

[129] *N.Y. Educ. Law* Sec. 236 (McKinney 1969).

[130] *Ibid.*, Sec. 236(3,8).

[131] *Ibid.*, Sec. 213(4).

[132] *Ibid.*

[133] *Ibid.*, Sec. 213(2).

[134] See prefatory note to *Cal. Educ. Code* Sec. 893.20 (West Supp. 1972).

[135] *Cal. Gov't Code* Sec. 14716 (West Supp. 1972).

[136] *Ibid.*, Sec. 14716.1.

[137] *Ibid.*, Sec. 14716.2.

[138] *Ibid.*

[139] *Cal. Educ. Code* Sections 893.20, .21 (West Supp. 1972).

[140] *Ibid.*

[141] *Vt. Stat. Ann.* tit. 16, Sec. 2802 (1968).

[142] *Ibid.*, Sec. 2804.

[143] *Ibid.*, Sec. 2805.

[144] *N.M. Stat. Ann.* Sections 73-26-34, 35 (Supp. 1971).

[145] Me. Rev. Stat. Ann. tit. 20, Sec. 2601 (Supp. 1972).

[146] Following the method outlined in Chapter II, no statutes on educational broadcasting were found in the official compilations of state laws for eleven states: Arizona, Colorado, Connecticut, Hawaii, Idaho, Indiana, Kansas, Minnesota, Missouri, New Hampshire, and Texas. Statutes on educational broadcasting in Illinois, Michigan, North Carolina, and Wyoming deal with commissions that have expired or not yet fully materialized. See Ill. Ann. Stat. ch. 122, Sec. 851 et seq. (Smith-Hurd Supp. 1972); Mich. Comp. Laws Ann. Sec. 388.1041 et seq. (1967); N.C. Gen. Stat. Sec. 115-78(e) (repl. 1966); and Wyo. Stat. Ann. Sec. 9-220.1 et seq. (Supp. 1971).

[147] Mont. Rev. Codes Ann. Sec. 75-5710 (2d repl. 1971).

[148] Ibid.

[149] Ibid., Sec. 75-5711.

[150] Fla. Stat. Ann. Sec. 229.805(5) (Supp. 1972).

[151] N.Y. Educ. Law Sec. 236(7) (McKinney 1969).

[152] R.I. Gen. Laws Ann. Sec. 16-28-3 (Reenactment of 1969).

[153] 53:503, RR (See Current Service Volumes); 47 CFR 73.503.

[154] 53:621, RR (See Current Service Volumes); 47 CFR 73.621.

[155] 53:503, RR; 47 CFR 73.503.

[156] 53:621, RR; 47 CFR 73.621.

[157] Okla. Stat. Ann. tit. 70, Sec. 23-102 (Supp. 1971).

[158] R.I. Gen. Laws Ann. Sec. 16-28-3 (Reenactment of 1969).

[159] Ala. Code tit. 52, Sec. 628 (1960).

[160] Ark. Stat. Ann. Sec. 80-3902 (Supp. 1971).

[161] La. Rev. Stat. Ann. Sec. 17:2503(D) (Supp. 1972).

[162]*Ibid.*

[163]*N.Y. Educ. Law* Sec. 236(7) (McKinney 1969).

[164]*Ky. Rev. Stat. Ann.* Sec. 168.100 (Baldwin's Supp. 1971).

[165]*Mass. Gen. Laws Ann.* ch. 71, Sec. 13I (1969).

[166]*Neb. Rev. Stat.* Sec. 79-2103(9) (1971).

[167]*Miss. Code Ann.* Sec. 8946-108 (Supp. 1971).

[168]For further information about this organization, see *Encyclopedia of Associations*, 5th ed. (Detroit: Book Tower, 1968), p. 570.

[169]Louisiana, Maryland, Mississippi, Nebraska, New Jersey, South Carolina, and South Dakota.

[170]47 U.S.C.A. Sec. 399 (Supp. 1972).

[171]47 U.S.C.A. Sec. 398 (Supp. 1972).

[172]47 U.S.C.A. Sec. 307 (1962)

[173]*State of Maine v. University of Maine*, Me., 266 A.2d 863, 868 (1970).

[174]*Ibid.*

[175]The Maine statute was a verbatim copy of the following Florida law, cited as *Fla. Stat. Ann.* Sec. 246.13 (1961): "None of the facilities, plant or personnel of any educational television system which is supported in whole or in part by state funds shall be used directly or indirectly for the promotion, advertisement or advancement of any political candidate for any municipal, county or state office; or for the purpose of advocating or opposing any specific program, existing or proposed, of governmental action which shall include, but shall not be limited to, constitutional amendments; tax referendums; or bond issues. Conviction upon violation of any provision of this section shall be punishable by not more than 1 year in prison or $5,000.00 fine, or both such fine and imprisonment." Note that the penalty provision in the above Florida statute was not adopted verbatim in the Maine statute.

[176]*Me. Rev. Stat. Ann.* tit. 20, Sec. 2606 (1964). For an interesting discussion of the legislative history of this statute, see Note, "Maine's Educational Television Network: Legal Difficulties," 22 *Maine Law Review* 239 (1970).

[177]Me., 266 A.2d 863, 866 (1970).

[178]*Ibid.*, p. 868.

[179]*Ibid.*, p. 869.

[180]*Me. Rev. Stat. Ann.* tit. 20, Sec. 2606 (Supp. 1972).

[181]*Fla. Stat. Ann.* Sec. 246.13 (1967).

[182]*Fla. Stat. Ann.* Sec. 229.805(5a) (Supp. 1972).

[183]Florida, Kentucky, Louisiana, Maine, Maryland, Massachusetts, New Jersey, New York, Oklahoma, and Rhode Island.

[184]Nebraska, Pennsylvania, and South Dakota.

[185]Louisiana, Maryland, Nebraska, Oklahoma, Oregon, Rhode Island, and South Dakota.

[186]Me., 266 A.2d 863, 868 (1970).

[187]Walter B. Emery, "Is There a Constitutional Flaw In the Public Broadcasting Act of 1967?," *Educational Broadcasting Review*, II (February 1968), 20.

[188]*Ibid.*

[189]*Ibid.*

[190]*Mayflower Broadcasting Corporation*, 8 F.C.C. 333 (1940).

[191]Daniel W. Toohey, "The Avoidance of Offense: Observations on the Matter of Broadcast Censorship," 15 *Saint Louis University Law Journal* 48, 54 (1970).

[192]*Editorializing By Broadcast Licensees*, 13 F.C.C. 1246 (1949).

CHAPTER V

BROADCASTING AND ADVERTISING

The primary responsibility for the regulation and control of all forms of advertising in the United States is vested in the Federal Trade Commission[1] which enforces the provisions of the Federal Trade Commission Act of 1914.[2] Though the FTC Act, as originally enacted, was not intended to deal with the problems of false advertising,[3] an early (1922) U.S. Supreme Court decision established beyond doubt that Federal Trade Commission jurisdiction in the field was indisputable.[4] Subsequent court decisions prompted later Congressional amendments to the Federal Trade Commission Act which widened the FTC's jurisdictional basis and provided for broader enforcement powers for Commission action concerning false advertising.[5]

However, the Federal Trade Commissions's jurisdictional basis has not been so widened as to exclude and preempt state regulatory activity in the advertising field, witness the opinion of a United States District Court:

> No such clear statement of Congressional intent of uniform federal standards is found in the Federal Trade Commission Act. Neither in its text nor in its legislative history is

> there anything to indicate an intention by the Congress to confer exclusive jurisdiction on the Federal Trade Commission.[6]

Indeed, the Federal Trade Commission itself has encouraged state regulatory activity in the advertising field.[7] The states have responded to such encouragement and today have statutes that 1) complement and extend federal legislation and, 2) deal with the advertising of specific commodities.

State statutes on advertising discussed in this chapter are organized into two major categories. One category contains statutes that deal with <u>general</u> legal controls over fraudulent advertising, deceptive trade practices, and consumer fraud practices. The second major category contains statutes on <u>specific</u> legal controls. Statutes in this second category cover foods, drugs, and cosmetics, political advertising, and the dissemination of fraudulent and deceptive advertisements of commodities such as insurance, loans, and real estate. Other statutory laws regulate professional occupations, such as dentistry, law, and psychology. Miscellaneous statutes which are also included in this second category deal with such topics as securities, liquor, bingo, cemetery lots, and apples.

General Legal Controls

Thirty-four states have enacted statutes that cover one or more areas in this category of general legal controls. Twenty-one states have fraudulent advertising statutes based on the *Printers' Ink* model statute; five states have adopted the Uniform Deceptive Trade Practices Act; and sixteen states have incorporated deceptive advertising provisions as part of more general consumer fraud statutes. Nine states have enacted statutes in two of these three areas, but Illinois is the only one to have enacted statutes in all three. Table 4 at the end of this dissertation lists the states that have enacted laws in each of these three areas.

Fraudulent Advertising

One of the earliest actions by the states to regulate fraudulent advertising came in response to a three-part article published in 1911 in *Printers' Ink*, a journal for advertisers.[8] In its November 23, 1911 issue, *Printers' Ink* published a model statute which the journal recommended for enactment by the states to assist them in eliminating misleading and dishonest advertising.[9] This *Printers' Ink* model statute reads as follows:

> Any person, firm, corporation or association who, with intent to sell or in any wise dispose of merchandise, securities, service, or anything offered by such person, firm, corporation or association, directly or indirectly, to the public for sale or distribution, or with intent to increase the consumption thereof, or to induce the public in any manner to enter into any obligation relating thereto, or to acquire title thereto, or an interest therein, makes, publishes, disseminates, circulates, or places before the public, or causes, directly or

> indirectly, to be made, published, disseminated, circulated, or placed before the public, in this State, in a newspaper or other publication, or in the form of a book, notice, hand-bill, poster, bill, circular, pamphlet, or letter, or in any other way, an advertisement of any sort regarding merchandise, securities, service, or anything so offered to the public, which advertisement contains any assertion, representation or statement of fact which is untrue, deceptive or misleading, shall be guilty of a misdemeanor.[10]

In 1945 the _Printers' Ink_ statute was revised and approved by the National Association of Better Business Bureaus.[11]

The _Printers' Ink_ model statute has been adopted in some form in twenty-one states.[12] These model statutes are, properly, aimed at advertisers rather than disseminators of advertisements. However, neither the original nor revised version of the _Printers' Ink_ statute contains provisions that specifically exempt the media from prosecution if they carry any "untrue, deceptive or misleading" advertisement.

To remedy this situation, thirteen of the twenty-one states have attached a provision to their _Printers' Ink_ statutes that relieves broadcasters from responsibility for broadcasting a fraudulent advertisement produced by any person, firm, corporation, or association.[13] However, eleven of these thirteen states qualify this exemption to relieve broadcasters from liability provided they broadcast such an advertisement "in good faith and without knowledge" of its false, deceptive, or misleading character.[14] Statutes in two states, Arkansas[15] and New York,[16] do not contain this qualifier and thus protect the broadcaster more absolutely.

Statutes in the eight remaining states with fraudulent advertising laws modeled after Printers' Ink do not stipulate any exemptions for broadcasters.[17] Indeed, the Hawaii statute specifically exempts any owner or publisher of a "newspaper," while "broadcasters" are conspicuously absent from the law.[18] Such an omission on Hawaii's part would be understandable if the law was never amended since its original enactment date of 1925. However, the omission is difficult to understand since Hawaii's statute has been amended in 1935, 1941, 1945, 1955, and 1963. It appears that the omission is intentional. Clearly, broadcasters are at a disadvantage in those states in which they are denied statutory protections afforded others. A possible consequent of such denial is that courts could hold broadcasters liable for disseminating fraudulent advertisements. This disadvantageous position for broadcasters could be rectified if all states adopted the qualified statutory exemption as discussed above. This position and reasons for such adoption are further explicated in Chapter VII.

While not specifically delineating "broadcasters" as exempt from liability, the Virginia statutes state that "a person, firm, corporation or association" that distributes any advertisement for compensation, does not violate the provisions of the false advertising statute if "the copy or information" supplied by the advertiser was relied upon.[19]

In addition to the twenty-one states discussed above, Indiana[20] and New Mexico[21] have enacted legislation that deals with fraudulent advertising, but these statutes do not appear to be based on provisions set forth in the *Printers' Ink* model statute. Michigan[22] and New York[23] (two of the twenty-one states) also have enacted fraudulent advertising statutes not modeled after *Printers' Ink*. The essential difference between the statutes modeled after *Printers' Ink* and the statutes in two of these four states is that whereas the *Printers' Ink* statutes deal only with advertisements containing untrue, deceptive, or misleading representations of fact, the laws in New Mexico[24] and New York[25] expand the definition of fraudulent advertising to include the *failure to reveal material facts* in the light of such representations. While the Michigan statutes prohibit fraudulent advertising, they do not include the provision on omission of material facts, but do cover the advertising of *availability* of goods and the misrepresentation of available supply in relation to reasonably expectable public demand.[26] The Indiana statutes do not contain provisions concerning either the omission of material facts or the availability of goods. However, the Indiana statutes include door-to-door distribution as a form of dissemination through which fraudulent advertisements may be transmitted.[27] Inspection of the statutes in these four states shows some interstate influence, even though it has no relationship to the contiguity of the states. The New Mexico statutes are almost a verbatim copy of New York's laws passed two years earlier. These four fraudulent advertising statutes have relatively recent enactment dates (1963-1967) as contrasted with the twenty-one state statutes modeled after Printers' Ink. The enactment dates of the Printers' Ink statutes and subsequent modifications span several decades (1911-1967), with most broadcasting exemptions occurring between 1941-1957.

In order to better understand some of the reasons for these recent state statutes discussed above, expecially the development and enactment of those covering deceptive trade practices and consumer fraud practices, to be discussed later, it is necessary to look at the development of federal legislation over the same period of time during which most state legislation was enacted, i.e., between 1911-1967. It should be emphasized that initial legislation on the regulation of fraudulent advertising was enacted at the state level, subsequent to the 1911 publication of the Printers' Ink model statute. The initial thrust of federal legislation came in 1914 when Congress enacted the Federal Trade Commission Act. The FTC Act provided for the establishment of the Federal Trade

Commission, an administrative agency empowered to issue cease-and-desist orders against violations of the Act's specific proscription of "unfair methods of competition."[28] Rather than define or enumerate specific examples of "unfair methods of competition," Congress left the bounds of this general prohibition to be defined by the FTC.[29]

The first case to reach the courts from the new Federal Trade Commission came in 1919 and involved the regulation of advertising.[30] In _Sears, Roebuck & Co. v. FTC_,[31] the Circuit Court of Appeals for the Seventh Circuit upheld the FTC's power to control deception in advertising.[32] In 1922, the U.S. Supreme Court added its approval of such regulatory activity in the case _FTC v. Winsted Hosiery Co._[33] However, in the 1931 case of _FTC v. Raladam Co._,[34] a formidable obstacle to FTC control over fraudulent advertising was presented by the U.S. Supreme Court's holding that the FTC must find that _competitors_ and not merely _consumers_ were injured by the misrepresentation.[35]

Congress acted to remove this obstacle by amending the Federal Trade Commission Act vis-a-vis the Wheeler-Lea Act of 1938.[36] The Wheeler-Lea Act added to the general proscription of "unfair methods of competition" a prohibition of "unfair or deceptive acts or practices."[37] This action on the part of Congress placed the interest of the consumer in protection against deception on an equal basis with the interest of competitors in fair trade practices.[38] The Wheeler-Lea Act also expanded the means by which the FTC could combat advertising dangerous to public health.[39] (This part of the Wheeler-Lea amendments will be discussed later under the category of "Specific Legal Controls" concerning food and drug advertising.)

In protecting the consumer against deceptive advertisements, the Wheeler-Lea amendments made possible more vigorous FTC action against a wide range of deceptive practices.[40] However, no provisions in the original FTC act nor in the Wheeler-Lea amendments required the affirmative disclosure of all material facts in an advertisement. Recognizing that suppressed truth may be as misleading as a false statement,[41] the FTC "developed a formula which will allow it to proceed against some misleadingly incomplete advertisements."[42] However, in the 1950 case of _Alberty_ v. _FTC_,[43] the United States Court of Appeals for the District of Columbia Circuit held that it was beyond the FTC's power to force an advertiser to be more informative.[44] The court held that the Federal Trade Commission had the function only of preventing falsity, not of improving the informativeness of advertising generally.[45] The court did not deny, however, that the FTC could act against _misrepresentation by silence_,[46] and therefore, "by finding that silence is deceptive in light of claims actually made, the Commission has been able to require increased affirmative disclosure of the limitations of a true claim without departing from the theory that it deals only with actively deceptive advertisements."[47]

Although the courts have generally upheld FTC findings that silence is deceptive,[48] the Federal Trade Commission still must view omission of material facts in advertising under the general proscription of "deceptive acts or practices" as stipulated in the Wheeler-Lea Act.

Perhaps this lack of specificity in the federal law accounts for recent state legislation which includes "omission of material facts" as part of the provisions concerning deceptive trade practices and consumer fraud practices. Clearly then, these recent state statutes go beyond the federal law in defining deceptive advertising.

The fact that the Federal Trade Commission cannot require advertisements to be more informative is further qualified by the Fair Packaging and Labeling Act,[49] which became effective July 1, 1967. This Act gives the FTC power to require affirmative disclosure of certain information on labels of consumer commodities, provided only that such information "facilitate value comparisons."[50]

Uniform Deceptive Trade Practices Act

Extensions and enlargements of general state fraudulent advertising statutes are contained in the Uniform Deceptive Trade Practices Act of 1964. This Act was adopted by Connecticut[51] and Delaware[52] in 1965; by Illinois[53] in 1966; by Florida[54] in 1967; and by Nebraska[55] in 1969. This Uniform Act, designed to update state laws in the field, represents a progressive forward step toward the objective of truth in advertising.[56]

In contrast to the generally-worded fraudulent advertising statutes modeled after Printers' Ink, provisions in the Uniform Deceptive Trade Practices Act stipulate specific objectionable practices.

> A person engages in a deceptive trade practice when, in the course of his business, vocation, or occupation, he:
>
> (1) Passes off goods or services as those of another;
> (2) Causes likelihood of confusion or of misunderstanding as to the source, sponsorship, approval, or certification of goods or services;
> (3) Causes likelihood of confusion or of misunderstanding as to affiliation, connection, or association with, or certification by, another;
> (4) Uses deceptive representations or designations of geographic origin in connection with goods or services;
> (5) Represents that goods or services have sponsorship, approval, characteristics, ingredients, uses, benefits, or quantities that they do not have, or that a person has a sponsorship, approval, status, affiliation, or connection that he does not have;
> (6) Represents that goods are original or new if they are deteriorated, altered, reconditioned, reclaimed, used, or second-hand;
> (7) Represents that goods or services are of a particular standard, quality, or grade, or that goods are of a particular style or model, if they are of another;
> (8) Disparages the goods, services, or business of another by false or misleading representation of fact;

(9) Advertises goods or services with intent not to sell them as advertised;
(10) Advertises goods or services with intent not to supply reasonably expectable public demand, unless the advertisement discloses a limitation of quantity;
(11) Makes false or misleading statements of fact concerning the reasons for, existence of, or amounts of, price reductions; or
(12) Engages in any other conduct which similarly creates a likelihood of confusion or of misunderstanding.[57]

It is interesting to note that provisions (9) and (10) are conspicuously absent from the Connecticut statutes,[58] and that provision (12) does not appear in the Florida laws.[59]

The deceptive practices singled out by the Uniform Act can roughly be divided into conduct involving either misleading trade identification, or fraudulent or deceptive advertising.[60] Contrary to the statutory provisions concerning false advertising, trade identification provisions[61] are presumably of remote interest to broadcasters who, in any event, are exempted from the Uniform Act's provisions in the five states which have this statute provided they disseminate the material "without knowledge of its deceptive character."

It should be pointed out that although certain deceptive trade practices are singled out in the Uniform Act, "courts are left free to fix the proper ambit of the Act in case-by-case adjudications."[62]

Consumer Fraud

The recent trends toward "consumerism" and protection of consumer interests in the United States are well-served by statutes in sixteen states[63] that deal with consumer protection from deceptive acts and practices. Statutes in these sixteen states differ from the fraudulent advertising statutes modeled after *Printers' Ink* in that the consumer fraud statutes generally comprise a comprehensive group of laws covering several unlawful practices, with only one statute in the group addressed specifically to fraudulent advertising.

Enactment of both consumer fraud and Uniform Deceptive Trade statutes has been a recent activity of state legislatures. Whereas the five Uniform Deceptive Trade statutes were enacted between 1965-1969, twelve of the sixteen states with consumer fraud statutes enacted theirs between 1967-1970.[64]

The distinguishing feature of the consumer fraud statutes is a provision that prohibits the "concealment, suppression, or omission of any material fact" in connection with any advertisement. The provisions in the following Delaware statute are representative of the provisions found in the consumer fraud statutes in all sixteen states.

(a) The act, use or employment by any person of any deception, fraud, false pretense, false promise, misrepresentation, or the concealment, suppression, or omission of any material fact with intent that others rely upon such concealment, suppression or omission, in connection with the sale or advertisement of any merchandise, whether or not any person has in fact been misled, deceived or damaged thereby, is an unlawful practice.

(b) This section shall not apply--

(1) to the owner or publisher of newspapers, magazines, publications or printed matter wherein such advertisement appears, or to the owner or operator of a radio or television station which disseminates such advertisement when the owner, publisher or operator has no knowledge of the intent, design or purpose of the advertiser; or

(2) to any advertisement or merchandising practice which is subject to and complies with the rules and regulations, of and the statutes administered by, the Federal Trade Commission.[65]

The provision exempting broadcasters from the law is found in all sixteen states. In fourteen of these states the qualifying provision is that the broadcaster have "no knowledge of the intent, design or purpose of the advertiser." Statutes in Minnesota[66] and New York[67] do not contain this "no knowledge" qualifier, and thus broadcasters are afforded absolute protection in those two states.

Provision (2) in the above Delaware law is another distinguishing feature common to the consumer fraud statutes. This provision in consumer fraud legislation at the state level is the first indication of the states' recognition of and willingness to complement the enforcement of federal statutes and decisions governing unfair or deceptive acts or practices in order to protect the public.[68]

Statutes in Illinois[69] and Kansas[70] extend the definition of the term "advertisement" to include "every work device to disguise any form of business solicitation by using such terms as 'renewal,' 'invoice,' 'bill,' 'statement,' or 'reminder,' to create an impression of existing obligation when there is none, or other language to mislead any person in relation to any sought after commercial transaction." The California Consumers Legal Remedies Act is unique among the consumer fraud statutes in these sixteen states in that the Act stipulates the remedies and procedures available to any consumer who suffers any damage as a result of the use by any person of a practice declared to be unlawful in the statutes.[71]

Although the statutes being discussed here are found under title headings of "consumer fraud" rather than "deceptive trade," the provisions in the statutes in two of the states, California[72] and Texas,[73] list several deceptive trade practices. These lists are almost verbatim copies of deceptive trade practices contained in the Uniform Deceptive Trade Practices Act. Thus, while some states have enacted consumer fraud legislation and others have enacted deceptive trade legislation, both types of legislation appear to cover the same ground under different names.

This matter of semantics also extends to the qualifying phrase that protects the broadcaster from liability for disseminating a deceptive advertisement. That is, in the statutes modeled after *Printers' Ink*, the qualifier is "in good faith"; under the Uniform Deceptive Trade Practices Act the qualifier is "without knowledge of its deceptive character"; and under consumer fraud legislation the qualifier is "no knowledge of the intent, design or purpose of the advertiser." It appears that all three types of legislation stipulate the same exemption in different words.

Specific Legal Controls

The second major category of advertising statutes that affect broadcasting includes all statutes that deal with specific persons and commodities. Statutes in this category cover foods, drugs, and cosmetics, political advertising, and commodities such as insurance, loans, and real estate. Other statutory laws regulate the advertising of certain professional occupations and miscellaneous items such as securities, liquor, bingo, cemetery lots, and apples.

Foods, Drugs, Cosmetics

An excellent example of states following the lead of federal legislation in a particular area is found in state laws governing food and drug regulation. Most state legislation on foods and drugs parallels provisions set forth in the Pure Food and Drug Act of 1906[74] and the federal Food, Drug, and Cosmetic Act of 1938.[75] The 1938 Act served as a model for the Association of Food and Drug Officials of the United States which drafted the Uniform State Food, Drug and Cosmetic Bill, cited as the State Food, Drug and Cosmetic Act.[76]

This Uniform State Food, Drug and Cosmetic Act goes beyond the federal Food, Drug and Cosmetic Act by prohibiting false advertising,[77] with the statutory guidelines paralleling the federal standard set forth in the Federal Trade Commission Act.[78] As a result of the Wheeler-Lea Act (discussed earlier), the Federal Trade Commission was given jurisdiction over fraudulent advertising of "foods, drugs, devices, or cosmetics."[79] "This allocation to the FTC of responsibility for subjects within the traditional jurisdiction of the Food and Drug Administration was the result of a legislative compromise."[80] Indeed, this apparent overlapping system of dual enforcement shared by the FDA and FTC was intentional.[81]

> Over the objection of congressmen who favored placing all responsibility for the protection of health interests in the FDA, the chairman of the House Commerce Committee devised the plan of giving the FTC power over food and drug advertising. Thus the FTC and the FDA both were given power over the distribution of deceptively promoted foods, drugs, medical devices, and cosmetics. By an informal working agreement, the FDA primarily controls labeling while the FTC confines its regulation to advertising by means other than labels.[82]

Seventeen states have enacted legislation that deals with food and drug advertising.[83] In all seventeen states a broadcaster is exempted from liability for disseminating a false advertisement, an exemption that parallels provisions in the federal law.[84] The following provisions in the Rhode Island law are typical of the nearly uniform provisions found in the statutes in these seventeen states.

> No publisher, radio-broadcast licensee, or agency or medium for the dissemination of an advertisement, except the manufacturer, packer, distributor, or seller of the article to which a false advertisement relates, shall be liable under this section by reason of the dissemination by him of such false advertisement, unless he has refused, on the request of the director of health to furnish the director of health the name and post office address of the manufacturer, packer, distributor, seller, or advertising agency, residing in the state of Rhode Island who causes him to disseminate such advertisement.[85]

The reader should note that the liability exemption for the broadcaster is a qualified one. That is, the statutory provisions exempt the broadcaster from liability provided he does not refuse to furnish the state health director with certain information. Statutes in only two of these seventeen states, Maryland[86] and Ohio,[87] do not contain this qualifier, and thus afford the broadcaster absolute protection.

Political Advertising

Free elections are a hallmark of American democracy for "apart from this activity of the people there is no way of distinguishing democracy from other forms of government."[88] Free election campaigning in the United States has increasingly become synonymous with the mass media, especially broadcasting. Indeed, the expenditures of campaign funds on television advertising alone attest to the politicians' belief in that medium's pervasive power as an informative and suasory political tool. As a move towards establishing equity among candidates as to the limits of broadcast campaign expenditures, Congress passed the Federal Election Campaign Act.[89] However, this Federal Act does not stand alone on the matter. Nine states[90] have enacted legislation that regulates certain aspects of broadcast political advertising. There are no commonalities among the statutes across these nine states. However, except for Mississippi (1935)[91] and Wisconsin (1951),[92] legislation on political advertising has been a relatively recent concern for state legislatures. Statutes on political advertising in seven of the nine states have been enacted and/or amended since 1960.

California's statutes are unique among these nine states in that they contain several provisions which provide a rationale for regulation of political advertising.[93] In noting that the major political parties have become an integral part of the American governmental system, and that regulation of these parties as to their structure, governing bodies, and functions by state governments is in the public interest, the California State Legislature declared that "the voting public is entitled to protection by law from deception in political campaigns in the same manner and for the same reasons that it is entitled to protection from deception by advertisers of commercial products."[94]

California's statutes, cited as the Truth in Endorsements Law, were first enacted in 1963 and later amended in 1967.[95] The statutes require that a "Notice to Voters" be read in full concerning any paid political advertisements (having reference to any candidate in the direct primary election) intended for broadcast by radio or television. This "Notice to Voters" (which is also required by law to be printed on the page containing any printed political advertisement) reads as follows:

> The endorsement hereon is by an unofficial political group. Official organizations of the (name) Party are prohibited by law from endorsing candidates in primary elections.[96]

There are a few minor inconsistencies among the political advertising statutes in these nine states.

Broadcasters in Arizona,[97] Ohio,[98] and Texas[99] are required to keep a record for public inspection of certain information concerning political advertisements broadcast over their stations. Such information usually includes the name(s) and address(es) of the person(s) responsible for the advertisement. The Arizona statutes pertain to advertisements "in favor of or against an initiated or referred measure or amendment to the [state] constitution."[100] Ohio's laws pertain to candidates and issues,[101] while the statutes in Texas pertain to "political advertising" in general.[102] Such records must be kept for a period of six months in Ohio and Texas, whereas no time period is stipulated in Arizona's statutes. Although statutes in Kentucky do not require broadcasters to maintain records on political advertising, they do make such demands on newspapers and magazines.[103] These records must be kept for a period of one year, and shall include "all statements, articles, or advertisements" pertaining to "the support or defeat of a candidate or group of candidates for nomination or election to any public office."[104]

Kentucky statutes require all television and radio political announcements pertaining to candidates to be identified by the words "paid for by," followed by the name and address of the purchaser of the announcement.[105] Wisconsin[106] and Mississippi[107] have enacted similar legislation. The Mississippi statutes also contain a provision that prohibits any person from publishing any advertisement designed to influence voters for or against any candidate unless the advertisement "shall have been submitted to, and approved and subscribed by the candidate."[108] This provision is visionary in a sense since it is similar to one contained in the Federal Election Campaign Act (effective April 7, 1972) which requires candidate approval of advertisements. The Mississippi laws were enacted in 1935! Broadcasters in Virginia are required to report to the State Board of Elections the name and address of the person or persons who paid for political advertisements broadcast over their stations.[109] This report must be made within thirty days after an election, and must also include the amount of the cost of the advertisement.[110]

Statutes in Alaska make it a misdemeanor for anyone who knowingly makes a radio broadcast containing a false statement, charge, or comment relating to a political candidate or to an election proposition or question.[111]

Insurance

State statutes that define unfair and deceptive acts or practices in the business of insurance reflect the powers and privileges available to the states by virtue of Public Law 15, Chapter 20, Sec. 340, enacted by the 1st Session of the 79th Congress of the United States on March 9, 1945.[112] In this Public Law Congress declared that regulation and taxation by the states of the business of insurance is in the public interest, and that Congressional silence on the matter "shall not be construed to impose any barrier to the regulation or taxation of such business by the several States."[113] Congress went on to say in Public Law 15 that "the business of insurance, and every person engaged therein, shall be subject to the laws of the several States which relate to the regulation or taxation of such business."[114]

Ten states have enacted statutes that prohibit the disseminating of deceptive or misleading advertisements relating to the business of domestic insurance.[115] "Domestic" means that such insurance companies are authorized to do business in a given state.

The Illinois statutes are noteworthy in two respects among the statutes enacted by these ten states. First, the Illinois statutes preceded Congressional action in Public Law 15, having been enacted in 1937 and later amended in 1943.[116] Second, a provision in the Illinois statutes makes it unlawful for an insurance company to imply in its broadcast advertisements that the company, its financial condition, or status, "are approved, endorsed, or guaranteed by the State of Illinois or United States Government."[117]

The foregoing discussion dealt with statutes applicable to insurers authorized to do business in a given state, i.e., domestic insurers. Insurers who are not authorized to transact business in a given state are also subject to statutory laws in seven states. These seven states (included among the ten domestic insurance states) are Hawaii, Louisiana, Massachusetts, Minnesota, Nevada, Pennsylvania, and Wisconsin. These unauthorized insurers, who nevertheless may be authorized in another state, are sometimes called "foreign" or "alien" insurers in the statutes in the above seven states.

In Louisiana,[118] Minnesota,[119] Nevada,[120] and Wisconsin[121] foreign insurers are subject to the jurisdiction of the commissioner of insurance of the state, and are prohibited from broadcasting fraudulent advertisements that misrepresent the company's financial condition, terms of its contracts, or benefits to be received. It is interesting to note that while statutes in these four states prohibit fraudulent advertising _by_ foreign insurers, statutes in Hawaii[122] and Massachusetts[123] prohibit any broadcast advertisement "for or on behalf" of any insurer not authorized to transact insurance in the state. Pennsylvania has a similar statute prohibiting any advertising unless the radio or television broadcasting company has in its possession "a true and attested or photostatic copy of a certificate of authority from the

Insurance Department" to the effect that the insurance company is authorized to transact business in the Commonwealth.[124]

Loans

State statutes that regulate false or misleading broadcast advertising of the rates, terms, and conditions of loans are of two general types. One type is comprised of those statutes that affect different kinds of loans, whereas the second type is comprised of statutes that affect different kinds of lending agencies. Since more of the regulatory activity deals with loans than with lending agencies, loan laws are discussed more fully in this section.

Thirteen states[125] have enacted statutes that regulate broadcast advertising of loans. Two of these thirteen states do not specify any particular kind of loan advertising that is prohibited. Rather, both Kansas[126] and Maryland[127] have generally-worded statutes that make it unlawful to broadcast "in any manner whatsoever" any false, misleading, or deceptive statement with regard to the rates, terms, or conditions of lending money. Maryland makes it a misdemeanor for "any person" who violates its statute.

The remaining eleven states apply the foregoing general statutory proscriptions against fraudulent advertising to particular kinds of loans. One such kind is "small loans," covered by statutes in four states. Statutes in Minnesota set the value of a small loan at "$900 or less,"[128] while Wisconsin law sets the value at "three hundred dollars or less."[129] In contrast, provisions in California's statutes regulating small loans[130] and in Mississippi's Small Loan Regulatory Act[131] do not specify any amount or value of what constitutes a small loan.

Another kind of loan advertising concerns debt management, covered by statutory laws in Connecticut, Nebraska, Oregon, and Utah. The wording of the statutes is almost verbatim in Connecticut,[132] Nebraska,[133] and Utah.[134] These statutes make it unlawful to advertise by broadcast any false, misleading, or deceptive statement "with regard to the services to be performed by the licensee or the charges to be made therefor." In Oregon, statutory provisions exempt the broadcasting station from liability for broadcasting an unlawful advertisement concerning debt consolidation, provided that the station broadcast the advertisement "in good faith without knowledge of its unlawful character."[135]

Provisions in the Delaware statutes also exempt the broadcasting station which unknowingly disseminates false or misleading advertising matter about secondary mortgage loans.[136]

Statutes regulating broadcast advertising of installment loans are found in Hawaii and Oklahoma. The Hawaii statutes require that in any broadcast advertisement which gives the down payment or the amount of installment payments for the retail installment sale of goods or services, the same advertisement must also give 1) the total sale price; 2) the period of time over which installment payments are to be made; and 3) the total amount of goods or services to which the total sale price relates.[137] Provisions in Oklahoma's statutes governing misleading advertising concerning the terms or conditions of consumer credit exempt "the owner or personnel . . . of any medium in which an advertisement appears or through which it is disseminated."[138]

Without question, the state of California has been the most active among all fifty states in passing legislation on all phases of broadcasting. And nowhere is California's role as legislative leader more apparent than in the regulation of various types of agencies that lend money. Of the five kinds of agencies discussed in this section, California has enacted laws that regulate four of them. California statutes prohibit the broadcasting of false, misleading, or deceptive advertisements by Industrial Loan Companies,[139] Personal Property Brokers,[140] Check Sellers and Cashers,[141] and domestic Savings and Loan Associations.[142] The state of Arizona has similar false advertising statutes that affect credit unions.[143]

Professions

The licensing and regulation of various professions is extended by some state legislatures to prohibit all advertising by members of certain professional occupations, or to prohibit only fraudulent advertising. Nine states have enacted statutory laws that prohibit broadcast advertising of any kind or character relating to persons practicing dentistry. These nine states are Illinois,[144] Iowa,[145] Kansas,[146] Maryland,[147] Massachusetts,[148] New York,[149] Oklahoma,[150] Pennsylvania,[151] and Texas.[152] These same statutes forbidding broadcast advertising by dentists also apply to dental hygienists in Iowa,[153] Massachusetts,[154] and Oklahoma.[155] In three states, Kansas,[156] Massachusetts,[157] and New York,[158] persons engaged in the business of constructing or repairing dentures, bridges, or other structures to be worn as substitutes for natural teeth are not allowed to advertise to the general public by the broadcasting medium. The state of Maryland is unique among this group of nine states, in that while broadcasts of educational programs by the dental division of the Maryland State Department of Health are allowed, no public school clinic, state institution, eleemosynary institution, or business corporation (which maintain clinics for pupils, inmates or employees) shall advertise "in any manner or by any method" anything related to the practice of dentistry.[159]

Other professional occupations in six states are also regulated in various ways by statutory law. Lawyers in California are prohibited from using radio to give advice or render opinions on specific legal problems,[160] while psychologists in the state of Washington cannot engage in individual diagnosis or treatment in the course of radio or television programs.[161] Hawaii does not allow any public media advertising by optometrists.[162] While barbers in Nebraska are permitted to advertise prices or services on radio or television, barber schools are prohibited from advertising "in any manner . . . that it renders barber service to the general public."[163] However, a barber school may advertise for students.

Fraudulent advertising is prohibited by electrologists in Massachusetts,[164] which also prohibits deceptive advertising by anyone selling eye glasses, lenses, or eye glass frames.[165] Connecticut has a statute that prohibits fraudulent broadcast advertising by retail druggists.[166]

Real Estate

Four states have enacted statutes that deal with false or misleading advertising of real estate. California's statutes make it unlawful to broadcast any false or misleading "statement, pictorial representation or sketch" in any advertisement about subdivided lands.[167] The California laws exempt the broadcaster from liability for broadcasting a false advertisement, unless he "has actual knowledge of the falsity thereof or has an interest either as an owner or agent in the subdivided lands so advertised."[168] Similar statutes in Connecticut exempt the broadcasting station or network of stations from liability for disseminating unlawful advertising of "any subdivision, lot, parcel or unit in any subdivision."[169] Unlike California's statutes, however, the Connecticut laws do not qualify this exemption by incorporating the "actual knowledge" provision, and thus afford the broadcaster absolute protection.

Florida's statutes make it unlawful to broadcast false or misleading information for the purpose of "inducing" any person "to purchase real estate located in the state."[170]

In New York, no offer to sell subdivided lands by means of broadcast advertising may be made unless a copy of the advertisement has first been filed with the Department of State.[171] A filing fee of five dollars for each radio advertisement and of twenty-five dollars "for each item of television" must accompany each such copy filed.[172] In addition, all advertisements must contain reference to this filing and indicate that a copy is available, upon request, from the subdivider.[173]

Miscellaneous

The following group of advertising statutes that affect broadcasting covers such diverse topics as securities, liquor, bingo, cemetery lots, and apples. Since there is no pattern to the content of these laws, nor is there any pattern among the states that regulate such advertising, I will discuss these statutes in the order of frequency across states.

Advertising of securities is regulated by statutes in Illinois,[174] Nevada,[175] New Jersey,[176] Oregon,[177] and Texas.[178] The term "security" or "securities" is defined by law to include shares of stock, various trust and mortgage certificates, notes, bonds, debentures, "or any other instrument commonly known as a security, whether similar to those herein referred to or not."[179] Provisions in these statutes make it unlawful for any person to broadcast by radio or television any advertising matter in connection with the sale of any security, unless a copy of the advertisement has been filed with the appropriate state administrator concerning such securities.[180]

Advertising of liquor is covered by statutory law in four states. In both Maine[181] and New Hampshire,[182] liquor may be advertised over television and radio, but such advertising is subject to regulations of the liquor commissions in those states. While a New Jersey law stipulates that the state liquor commissioner is empowered to make general rules and regulations concerning the sale and distribution of alcoholic beverages, it does not give any specifics dealing with the advertising of liquor over radio and television.[183] All outdoor advertising of liquor is prohibited within the state of Texas, but the term "outdoor advertising" does not include "advertising appearing on radio or television."[184] It should be noted that while liquor advertising is permitted by statutory law to some extent in these four states, provisions in both the Radio and Television Codes of the National Association of Broadcasters stipulate that the advertising of hard liquor is not acceptable.[185] However, these NAB Codes do not have the force of law and hence are not binding upon member stations nor, of course, upon stations that do not subscribe to the Codes.

Broadcast advertising of contraceptives is prohibited by statutory law in Delaware[186] and Utah.[187] The prohibition against public display of "explicit sexual materials" in Arizona does not apply to "broadcasts or telecasts through facilities licensed under the Federal Communications Act."[188]

Both Florida[189] and Virginia[190] have enacted religious discrimination statutes that make it unlawful to broadcast any commercial advertisement to the effect that the patronage of any person is not welcome, or is objectionable, at an establishment because of the person's religion. Virginia's law was enacted in 1954 and Florida's in 1955.

A contiguous states relationship exists between California and Nevada concerning their laws governing the adoption of children. The Nevada statute stipulates that a person or organization shall be guilty of a misdemeanor if he or it advertises that he or it will place children for adoption, or accept, supply, or provide children for adoption if that person or organization does not hold a "valid unrevoked license to place children for adoption issued by the welfare division of the department of health, welfare, and rehabilitation."[191] An almost verbatim copy of this Nevada statute has been adopted in California, effective July 1, 1973.[192]

Advertising of games of chance conducted under any license issued under New Jersey's Bingo Licensing Law is prohibited with regard to time and place of the event, and also to the prizes awarded.[193] New York has enacted a similar statute prohibiting the advertising of bingo games.[194] New Jersey's Raffles Licensing Law contains similar provisions that affect games of chance conducted under any license issued under that law.[195]

No person in Massachusetts may advertise goods imported from a foreign country unless such advertisement also contains the words "Imported Goods."[196] However, as used in this statute the word "person" does not include a person who owns and operates a radio or television station.[197] Advertisements of cemetery lots in New York must state the cemetery grounds location, including the city, town or village, and the county and state.[198]

In Oregon, all legally authorized city bonds must be advertised for sale at least once each week for not less than two successive weeks, and such advertising "may be broadcast or telecast on one or more local radio or television stations."[199] These same provisions also apply to Oregon's general obligation bonds.[200] Illinois imposes a fine and possible jail sentence upon any person who violates its abortion laws relating to the advertising for sale of any drug, medicine, instrument or other substance known to be an "abortifacient."[201]

Three states have enacted statutes pertaining to the advertising of agricultural products. Virginia's statute is a general proscription against "misrepresentative" advertising by broadcast of "any agricultural commodities."[202] In Nebraska, the Department of Agriculture is authorized to disseminate via broadcasts "timely reports of such information as will be of general value and benefit to the producers and dealers in poultry and eggs and will promote the general welfare of the poultry industry."[203] Finally, when apples are advertised for sale by radio or television in the state of Maine, advertisements in which prices are to be quoted, such advertisements "must state the correct grade, size and variety."[204]

FOOTNOTES

[1]15 U.S.C.A. Sec. 41 (1963).

[2]15 U.S.C.A. Sec. 45 et seq. (1963).

[3]Earl W. Kintner, "Federal Trade Commission Regulation of Advertising," 64 *Michigan Law Review* 1269, 1272-1273 (May 1966); see also Ira M. Millstein, "The Federal Trade Commission and False Advertising," 64 *Columbia Law Review* 439, 450 (1964).

[4]*Federal Trade Commission* v. *Winsted Hosiery Company*, 258 U.S. 483 (1922).

[5]The most important Congressional amendments were contained in the Wheeler-Lea Act, 52 Stat. 111 (1938). For information concerning additional amendments, see Kintner, pp. 1277-1278.

[6]*Double-Eagle Lubricants, Inc.* v. *Texas*, 248 F. Supp. 515, 518 (N.D. Texas, 1965).

[7]Note, "Developments in the Law--Deceptive Advertising," 80 *Harvard Law Review* 1005, 1135 (March 1967).

[8]The three-part article was written by the editor of *Printers' Ink*, John Irving Romer, and was entitled "Legal Repression of Dishonest Advertising." Part I appeared in the November 16, 1911 issue of *Printers' Ink*, pp. 3, 4, 6; Part II appeared in the November 23 issue, pp. 66, 68-70; and Part III was published in the November 30 issue, pp. 20, 22-23.

[9]*Printers' Ink*, November 23, 1911, p. 68.

[10]*Ibid*.

[11]For the complete text of the revised version of the *Printers' Ink* model statute, see Harold L. Nelson and Dwight L. Teeter, Jr., *Law of Mass Communications* (Mineola: The Foundation Press, Inc., 1969), pp. 455-456.

[12]See states listed under "Fraudulent Advertising--Printers' Ink" in Table 4 at the end of this dissertation.

[13]Arkansas, California, Connecticut, Georgia, Illinois, Maine, Massachusetts, Michigan, Missouri, Nevada, New York, Pennsylvania, and Wisconsin.

[14]California, Connecticut, Georgia, Illinois, Maine, Massachusetts, Michigan, Missouri, Nevada, Pennsylvania, and Wisconsin.

[15]Ark. Stat. Ann. Sec. 41-1963 (Supp. 1971).

[16]N.Y. Gen. Bus. Law Sec. 396(1) (McKinney 1968).

[17]Hawaii, Louisiana, Maryland, Minnesota, Tennessee, Utah, Virginia, and West Virginia.

[18]Hawaii Rev. Stat. Sec. 747-14 (1968).

[19]Va. Code Ann. Sec. 59.1-51 (repl. 1968).

[20]Ind. Ann. Stat. Sec. 10-3037 (IC 35-17-5-10) (Supp. 1971).

[21]N.M. Stat. Ann. Sections 49-12-2, 49-12-5.1 to 49-12-5.3 (Supp. 1971); Sections 49-12-1, 49-12-3 to 49-12-7 (repl. 1966).

[22]Mich. Comp. Laws Ann. Sec. 445.801 et seq. (1967).

[23]N.Y. Gen. Bus. Law Sec. 350 et seq. (McKinney 1968).

[24]N.M. Stat. Ann. Sec. 49-12-2 (Supp. 1971).

[25]N.Y. Gen. Bus. Law Sec. 350-a (McKinney 1968).

[26]Mich. Comp. Laws Ann. Sec. 445.801 (1967).

[27]Ind. Ann. Stat. Sec. 10-3037 (IC 35-17-5-10) (Supp. 1971).

[28]38 Stat. 719 (1914).

[29]Harvard Law Review, supra note 7, pp. 1019-1020.

[30]Ibid., p. 1020.

[31]258 F. 307 (7th Cir. 1919).

[32]*Ibid*.

[33]258 U.S. 483 (1922).

[34]283 U.S. 643 (1931).

[35]*Ibid*.

[36]52 Stat. 111 (1938).

[37]*Ibid*.

[38]*Harvard Law Review*, *supra* note 7, p. 1021.

[39]52 Stat. 116 (1938).

[40]*Harvard Law Review*, *supra* note 7, p. 1021.

[41]*Ibid*., p. 1026.

[42]*Ibid*., p. 1048.

[43]182 F.2d 36 (D.C. Cir. 1950), *cert*. *denied*, 340 U.S. 818 (1950).

[44]*Harvard Law Review*, *supra* note 7, p. 1048.

[45]*Ibid*.

[46]*Ibid*.

[47]*Ibid*., pp. 1048-1049.

[48]*Ibid*., p. 1051.

[49]Public Law No. 89-755, 80 Stat. 1296 (1966).

[50]*Ibid*.

[51]*Conn*. *Gen*. *Stat*. *Ann*. Sec. 42-115c et seq. (Supp. 1971).

[52]*Del*. *Code* *Ann*. tit. 6, Sec. 2531 et seq. (Supp. 1970).

[53]*Ill*. *Ann*. *Stat*. ch. 121 1/2, Sec. 311 et seq. (Smith-Hurd Supp. 1972).

[54]*Fla*. *Stat*. *Ann*. Sec. 817.69 et seq. (Supp. 1972).

[55]*Neb*. *Rev*. *Stat*. Sec. 87-301 et seq. (1971).

[56]For an interesting discussion of the events that led to the drafting of the Uniform Deceptive Trade Practices Act by the National Conference of Commissioners on Uniform State Laws, see "Prefatory Notes," Ill. Ann. Stat. ch. 121 1/2, Sec. 311 et seq. (Smith-Hurd Supp. 1972).

[57]Del. Code Ann. tit. 6, Sec. 2532 (Supp. 1970).

[58]Conn. Gen. Stat. Ann. Sec. 42-115d (Supp. 1971).

[59]Fla. Stat. Ann. Sec. 817.71 (Supp. 1972).

[60]See "Prefatory Notes," Ill. Ann. Stat. ch. 121 1/2, Sec. 311 et seq. (Smith-Hurd Supp. 1972).

[61]Kan. Stat. Ann. Sec. 81-111 et seq. (1964).

[62]See "Prefatory Notes," Ill. Ann. Stat. ch. 121 1/2, Sec. 311 et seq. (Smith-Hurd Supp. 1972).

[63]See states listed under "Consumer Fraud" in Table 4 at the end of this dissertation.

[64]Arizona, Arkansas, California, Kansas, Maryland, Minnesota, Missouri, New Jersey, New York, North Carolina, Texas, and Vermont.

[65]Del. Code Ann. tit. 6, Sec. 2513 (Supp. 1970).

[66]Minn. Stat. Ann. Sec. 325.79 (Supp. 1971).

[67]N.Y. Gen. Bus. Law Sec. 349 (McKinney Supp. 1971).

[68]Vt. Stat. Ann. tit. 9, Sec. 2451 (1970-71).

[69]Ill. Ann. Stat. ch. 121 1/2, Sec. 261(a) (Smith-Hurd Supp. 1972).

[70]Kan. Stat. Ann. Sec. 50-601(a) (Supp. 1968).

[71]Cal. Civ. Code Sec. 1750 et seq. (West Supp. 1972).

[72]Ibid., Sec. 1770.

[73]Tex. Rev. Civ. Stat. Ann. art. 5069-10.01 (Vernon's 1971).

[74]34 Stat. 768 (1906).

[75]21 U.S.C.A. Sec. 301 et seq. (1961); see also Harvard Law Review, supra note 7, p. 1121.

[76] [All States] *Food Drug Cosmetic Law Reporter*, 10,101-10,125 (1964, revised 1969); see also *Harvard Law Review*, *supra* note 7, p. 1121.

[77] *Harvard Law Review*, *supra* note 7, p. 1121.

[78] 15 U.S.C.A. Sec. 55(a)(1) (1963).

[79] 15 U.S.C.A. Sec. 52 (1963).

[80] *Harvard Law Review*, *supra* note 7, p. 1021.

[81] See Kintner, *supra* note 3, p. 1276.

[82] *Harvard Law Review*, *supra* note 7, p. 1021.

[83] See states listed under "Foods, Drugs, Cosmetics" in Table 4 at the end of this dissertation.

[84] 15 U.S.C.A. Sec. 54(b) (1963).

[85] *R. I. Gen. Laws Ann.* Sec. 21-31-5 (Reenactment of 1968).

[86] *Md. Ann. Code* art. 43, Sec. 187D (Supp. 1971).

[87] *Ohio Rev. Code Ann.* Sec. 3715.54(B) (Page 1971).

[88] R. M. MacIver, "The Role of the People," in *Basic Issues of American Democracy*, eds. Hillman M. Bishop and Samuel Hendel (New York: Appleton-Century-Crofts, 1965), p. 13.

[89] The Federal Election Campaign Act became effective April 7, 1972.

[90] See states listed under "Political Advertising" in Table 4 at the end of this dissertation.

[91] *Miss. Code Ann.* Sec. 3176 (1957).

[92] *Wis. Stat. Ann.* Sections 12.14, 12.15 (1967).

[93] *Cal. Elections Code* Sec. 11701 (West Supp. 1972).

[94] *Ibid.*

[95] *Ibid.*, Sec. 11700.

[96] *Ibid.*, Sec. 11703.

[97] *Ariz. Rev. Stat. Ann.* Sec. 19-128(B) (Supp. 1971).

[98] *Ohio Rev. Code Ann.* Sec. 3599.09 (Page Supp. 1970).

[99] *Tex. Election Code Ann.* art. 14.10(b) (Vernon's Supp. 1971).

[100] *Ariz. Rev. Stat. Ann.* Sec. 19-128(B) (Supp. 1971).

[101] *Ohio Rev. Code Ann.* Sec. 3599.09(B) (Page Supp. 1970).

[102] *Tex. Election Code Ann.* art. 14.10(b) (Vernon's Supp. 1971).

[103] *Ky. Rev. Stat. Ann.* Sec. 123.095 (Baldwin's Supp. 1971).

[104] *Ibid.*

[105] *Ibid.*

[106] *Wis. Stat. Ann.* Sections 12.14, 12.15 (1967).

[107] *Miss. Code Ann.* Sec. 3176 (1957).

[108] *Ibid.*

[109] *Va. Code Ann.* Sec. 24.1-259 (Supp. 1971).

[110] *Ibid.*

[111] *Alaska Stat.* Sec. 15.55.040 (1971).

[112] 59 Stat. 33 (1945), as amended, 15 U.S.C.A. Sec. 1011 et seq. (1963).

[113] 15 U.S.C.A. Sec. 1011 (1963).

[114] *Ibid.*, Sec. 1012.

[115] See states listed under "Insurance--Domestic" in Table 4 at the end of this dissertation.

[116] *Ill. Ann. Stat.* ch. 73, Sec. 761 (Smith-Hurd 1965).

[117] *Ibid.*

[118] *La. Rev. Stat. Ann.* Sec. 22:1231 et seq. (Supp. 1972).

[119]Minn. Stat. Ann. Sec. 72A.33 et seq. (1968).

[120]Nev. Rev. Stat. Sec. 686.480 (1967).

[121]Wis. Stat. Ann. Sec. 207.04 (Supp. 1971).

[122]Hawaii Rev. Stat. Sec. 431-327 (1968).

[123]Mass. Gen. Laws Ann. ch. 175, Sec. 160A (1958).

[124]Pa. Stat. Ann. tit. 18, Sec. 4689 (1963).

[125]See states listed under "Loans" in Table 4 at the end of this dissertation.

[126]Kan. Stat. Ann. Sec. 16-418 (1964).

[127]Md. Ann. Code art. 58A, Sec. 15 (repl. 1972).

[128]Minn. Stat. Ann. Sec. 56.12 (1970).

[129]Wis. Stat. Ann. Sec. 214.16 (1957).

[130]Cal. Fin. Code Sec. 24410 (West 1968).

[131]Miss. Code Ann. Sec. 5591-05 (Supp. 1971).

[132]Conn. Gen. Stat. Ann. Sec. 36-376 (1969).

[133]Neb. Rev. Stat. Sec. 69-1214 (1971).

[134]Utah Code Ann. Sec. 58-30-13 (repl. 1963).

[135]Ore. Rev. Stat. Sec. 697.790 (1971).

[136]Del. Code Ann. tit. 5, Sec. 3127 (Supp. 1970).

[137]Hawaii Rev. Stat. Sec. 476-35 (1968).

[138]Okla. Stat. Ann. tit. 14A, Sec. 2-313 (Supp. 1971).

[139]Cal. Fin. Code Sec. 18617 (West Supp. 1972).

[140]Cal. Fin. Code Sec. 22000 et seq. (West 1968).

[141]Ibid., Sec. 12300 et seq.

[142]Ibid., Sec. 5050 et seq.

[143]Ariz. Rev. Stat. Ann. Sec. 6-535 (Supp. 1971).

[144] Ill. Ann. Stat. ch. 91, Sec. 62 (Smith-Hurd Supp. 1972).

[145] Iowa Code Ann. Sec. 153.32 (Supp. 1972).

[146] Kan. Stat. Ann. Sec. 65-1423 (Supp. 1968).

[147] Md. Ann. Code art. 32, Sec. 18 (repl. 1971).

[148] Mass. Gen. Laws Ann. ch. 112, Sec. 52A (1971).

[149] N.Y. Gen. Bus. Law Sec. 396-c (McKinney 1968).

[150] Okla. Stat. Ann. tit. 59, Sec. 328.28 (1971).

[151] Pa. Stat. Ann. tit. 63, Sec. 122 (1968).

[152] Tex. Penal Code Ann. art. 752a,b (Vernon's 1961).

[153] Iowa Code Ann. Sec. 153.32 (Supp. 1972).

[154] Mass. Gen. Laws Ann. ch. 112, Sec. 52A (1971).

[155] Okla. Stat. Ann. tit. 59, Sec. 328.29 (1971).

[156] Kan. Stat. Ann. Sec. 65-1423 (Supp. 1968).

[157] Mass. Gen. Laws Ann. ch. 112, Sec. 52C (1971).

[158] N.Y. Gen. Bus. Law Sec. 396-c (McKinney 1968).

[159] Md. Ann. Code art. 32, Sec. 18 (repl. 1971).

[160] Cal. Bus. & Prof. Code Sec. 6076, rule 18 (West 1962).

[161] Wash. Rev. Code Ann. Sec. 18.83.120 (Supp. 1971).

[162] Hawaii Rev. Stat. Sec. 459-9 (1968).

[163] Neb. Rev. Stat. Sec. 71-223.02 (1971).

[164] Mass. Gen. Laws Ann. ch. 112, Sec. 87KKK (1971).

[165] Mass. Gen. Laws Ann. ch. 112, Sec. 73A (1971).

[166] Conn. Gen. Stat. Ann. Sec. 19-241 (1969).

[167] Cal. Bus. & Prof. Code Sec. 11022 (West 1964).

[168] Ibid.

[169] Conn. Gen. Stat. Ann. Sec. 20-329k (Supp. 1971).

[170] Fla. Stat. Ann. Sec. 475.47 (1965).

[171] N.Y. Real Prop. Law Sec. 337-b(3) (McKinney Supp. 1971).

[172] Ibid.

[173] Ibid.

[174] Ill. Ann. Stat. ch. 121 1/2, Sec. 137.9 (Smith-Hurd 1960).

[175] Nev. Rev. Stat. Sec. 90.140 (1971); Sec. 90.210 (1969).

[176] N.J. Stat. Ann. Sec. 49:3-33 (1970).

[177] Ore. Rev. Stat. Sec. 59.345 (1971).

[178] Tex. Rev. Civ. Stat. Ann. art. 581-22 (Vernon's 1964).

[179] Ibid., art. 581-4.

[180] Ill. Ann. Stat. ch. 121 1/2, Sec. 137.9 (Smith-Hurd 1960).

[181] Me. Rev. Stat. Ann. tit. 28, Sec. 5 (1964).

[182] N.H. Rev. Stat. Ann. Sec. 175:10 (Supp. 1971).

[183] N.J. Stat. Ann. Sec. 33:1-39 (Supp. 1971).

[184] Tex. Penal Code Ann. art. 667-24a(1) (Vernon's 1952).

[185] NAB Television Code, Sixteenth Edition, IX.6 (April 1972); NAB Radio Code, Seventeenth Edition, II.C.1 (April 1972).

[186] Del. Code Ann. tit. 16, Sec. 2502 (1953).

[187] Utah Code Ann. Sec. 58-19-10 (repl. 1963).

[188] Ariz. Rev. Stat. Ann. Sec. 13-537 (Supp. 1971).

[189] Fla. Stat. Ann. Sec. 871.04 (1965).

[190] Va. Code Ann. Sec. 57-2.1 (repl. 1969).

[191]*Nev. Rev. Stat.* Sec. 127.310 (1967).

[192]*Cal. Civ. Code* Sec. 224p (West Supp. 1972).

[193]*N.J. Stat. Ann.* Sec. 5:8-36 (1959).

[194]*N.Y. Gen. Munic. Law* Sec. 490 (McKinney Supp. 1971).

[195]*N.J. Stat. Ann.* Sec. 5:8-63 (1959).

[196]*Mass. Gen. Laws Ann.* ch. 94, Sec. 277B (1972).

[197]*Ibid.*

[198]*N.Y. Gen. Bus. Law* Sec. 451 (McKinney 1968).

[199]*Ore. Rev. Stat.* Sec. 287.002 (1971).

[200]*Ibid.*, Sec. 552.660.

[201]*Ill. Ann. Stat.* ch. 38, Sections 23-2, 23-3 (Smith-Hurd 1970).

[202]*Va. Code Ann.* Sec. 59.1-54 (repl. 1968).

[203]*Neb. Rev. Stat.* Sec. 81-2,164.01 (1971).

[204]*Me. Rev. Stat. Ann.* tit. 7, Sec. 536 (1964).

CHAPTER VI

THE BUSINESS OF BROADCASTING

Owning and operating a broadcasting station is a business, and questions concerning the "public convenience, interest, or necessity"[1] become merely rhetorical if that business does not succeed.[2] State statutes governing business aspects of broadcasting are few in number, but diverse in the matters that are regulated. Table 5 at the end of the dissertation lists the states that have enacted laws on the various business aspects of broadcasting. This chapter will cover state laws that affect taxes, employment practices, and certain illegal activities such as the broadcasting of lotteries and gambling information. Miscellaneous topics covered by statutory law that do not fit into the above three categories will be discussed last. Since taxes receive more statutory attention than any other single aspect of the business of broadcasting, the tax statutes will be discussed fully.

Taxes

Two major types of state tax statutes affect broadcasters. One specifies certain taxes that broadcasters must pay; the second specifies certain taxes from which broadcasters are exempt. There are a few miscellaneous tax statutes that do not fit into either type.

Taxable Items

The most prevalent form of tax that broadcasters must pay is a "privilege" tax for doing business in the state. It should be noted that broadcasters, as a rule, are not singled out for this "privilege." Rather, these privilege taxes are generally applicable to most businesses, including newspapers. Five states have applied a privilege tax to broadcasting operations. In Delaware, a broadcasting station that operates with a power of more than 1,000 watts must pay an annual license tax of $300. A broadcasting station that operates with a power of 1,000 watts or less must pay an annual license tax of $150.[3]

Broadcasters in Arizona, Hawaii, Washington, and West Virginia are taxed a certain percentage of their gross annual income. Arizona levies an annual tax of 1 1/2 per cent of the gross proceeds of sales or gross income from advertising by radio or television.[4] The tax levied and collected under this Arizona statute is designated as the "special excise tax for education."[5] Hawaii levies an annual privilege tax upon broadcasting stations equal to 4 per cent of the gross income of the business.[6] The state of Washington levies an excise tax of .44 per cent of the gross income of broadcasting stations, "excluding network, national and regional advertising," and excluding "that portion of revenue represented by the out-of-state audience computed as a ratio to the station's total audience as measured by the 100 micro-volt signal strength and delivery by wire."[7] The gross income tax levied against broadcasters in West Virginia is equal to .71 per cent.[8]

In Maine, the sales and use tax law[9] has been amended by a 1966 Maine Supreme Court decision to include as taxable items a television station's preparation of art work and slides for an advertiser where the advertiser could determine if and when such slides would be broadcast.[10] Also, the passage of title to the slides to the advertiser at the end of a five-year period constitutes a "sale" within the meaning of Maine's Sales Tax Act.[11] However, the Maine Supreme Court also held that the selling of results of market surveys to television stations represented the performance of a service and such a transaction was not subject to Maine's use tax.[12]

Some comments are in order concerning the foregoing privilege taxes.[13] First, it is important to note that Delaware's annual license tax is levied against broadcasters, motion picture operators, and advertising agencies, but not against newspapers.[14] In Arizona[15] and Washington,[16] on the other hand, both broadcasters and publishers of newspapers are taxed. Second, the wording of these tax statutes raises some interesting questions about how state laws define a broadcasting station; Hawaii[17] and West Virginia[18] classify broadcasting stations along with theaters, opera houses, moving picture shows, vaudeville, amusement parks, dance halls, and skating rinks! West Virginia also classifies racetracks with the above sources of entertainment.

Tax Exemptions

Tax exemptions for broadcasters generally are exemptions from the state sales or use tax. Exceptions to this are a Texas statute which exempts church radio and television stations from property taxes,[19] and an Indiana statute which exempts broadcasting companies from the state's public utility tax.[20] Maryland prohibits any political subdivision of the state from imposing a gross receipts tax upon "each and every sale of time on or in connection with any radio or television broadcast originating in this State which time is used for advertising."[21]

Seven other states have enacted statutes that exempt all or part of the broadcaster's income from the state sales or use tax. Since there is no uniformity among these states' statutes, each exemption will be noted briefly.

In Florida charges for services rendered by broadcasting stations, including line charges, talent or license fees, and charges for films, video tapes, and transcriptions used in broadcast productions, are exempt from the state's sales tax law.[22] Similar laws in Mississippi exempt broadcasting stations from paying sales tax on the rental of films, video and audio tapes, and phonograph records.[23]

Broadcasting equipment and parts used by commercial radio and television companies in Virginia are exempted from the provisions of Virginia's Retail Sales and Use Tax Act.[24] South Carolina does not levy its sales tax on either the "gross proceeds of the sale of electricity to radio and television stations for use in producing programs," nor on the "gross proceeds of the sale of all supplies, technical equipment and machinery" used by stations in their productions.[25] It is interesting to note that for the purpose of this South Carolina statute, radio and television stations "shall be deemed to be manufacturers."[26]

In Hawaii state-fund-supported businesses organized for the purpose of broadcasting radio programs to areas outside Hawaii to promote tourism are exempt from the General Excise Tax Law.[27] A provision in New York's Tax Law statutes exempts "information services used by newspapers, radio broadcasters and television broadcasters in the collection and dissemination of news."[28]

In Michigan property purchased by persons licensed to operate commercial broadcasting stations is not subject to the statutory provisions of the Use Tax Act[29] and the General Sales Tax Act,[30] "when the property is used as a component part of a completed film, tape or recording produced for resale or transmission purposes."

Miscellaneous Tax Statutes

Miscellaneous tax laws include an Oklahoma statute that classifies radio broadcasting stations as "personal property" for taxation purposes.[31] A Texas statute allows a person broadcasting a record (under circumstances that require payment of a license or performing fee) to rely on the information shown on the label of the recording in the absence of a written note to the contrary.[32]

California has enacted a tax statute that stipulates:

> If the sale or exchange of property (including stock in a corporation) is certified by the Federal Communications Commission to be necessary or appropriate to effectuate a change in a policy of, or the adoption of a new policy by the commission with respect to the ownership and control of radio broadcasting stations, such sale or exchange shall, if the taxpayer so elects, be treated as an involuntary conversion of such property.[33]

Arizona[34] has enacted a similarly-worded tax law.

Employment Practices

In this category I will discuss those state statutory laws that govern various matters related to employment practices of broadcasting stations. These state statutes cover matters such as employment of minors, Sunday work hours, jury duty exemptions, and wages.

Employment Of Minors

The employment of minors by broadcasting stations is regulated by statutory law in six states: California, Florida, Maryland, Massachusetts, New York, and Wisconsin. Provisions in these laws generally specify the age of the minority, either under sixteen or eighteen years, and requirements such as parental or guardian consent, time of work, non-interference with schooling, and working conditions as typified by Maryland's provision that "the conditions of such employment are not detrimental to the health or morals of such minor."[35] Since the state statutes on employment of minors are dissimilar, each state will be discussed separately.

In California employment of minors in any radio or television broadcasting studio is permitted, providing that a written consent of the Labor Commissioner is first obtained.[36] This California statute does not stipulate whose responsibility it is to obtain such written consent. In contrast, Florida[37] and Maryland[38] statutes stipulate that it is the responsibility of the broadcasting station wishing to employ the minor to obtain permission from the proper commission. Broadcasters in Florida must make application to the Florida Industrial Commission for a permit that qualifies them to employ minors,[39] whereas broadcasters in Maryland must secure a similar permit from the Commissioner of the Department of Labor and Industry.[40]

The state of Massachusetts, in a 1935 amendment to its child labor laws, allows minors under sixteen years to be employed as talent in any radio broadcasting station.[41] Child performer laws in New York do not apply to minors providing they are employed "for not more than two hours a week" by a "regularly licensed broadcasting company, where the performance of the child . . . is of a non-professional character and occurs during hours when attendance for instruction is not required in accordance with the education law."[42] In addition, an application for a child performer permit giving general statements describing the part and the nature of the radio or television program must be filed with the Society for the Prevention of Cruelty to Children in New York City or, outside New York City, with the Society for the Prevention of Cruelty to Children.[43]

The state of Wisconsin permits minors under eighteen years "to appear for the purpose of singing, playing or performing" in any radio or television broadcast, and furthermore, does not require a labor permit for such employment.[44] However, other working conditions such as health and safety requirements must be met before a minor under eighteen years may be so employed.[45]

Sundays, Juries, Wages

The continuous daily operation of broadcasting stations accords the industry special status and exemptions from certain state regulations. For example, laws in Maine,[46] Massachusetts,[47] Mississippi,[48] and South Carolina[49] that prohibit business activities such as selling, advertising, and entertainment on Sunday, are not applicable to broadcasters in those states.

Persons in certain broadcast occupations are exempt from jury duty in four states. Alabama exempts "radio broadcasting engineers and announcers when engaged in the regular performance of their duties";[50] laws in Colorado exempt "editors and reporters when employed actively . . . in broadcasting";[51] Florida exempts "those who gather, prepare, edit and broadcast news for radio and television stations";[52] and Oklahoma exempts "persons actually engaged in the gathering or reporting of information for broadcasting or telecasting on news type programs."[53]

State minimum wage and overtime pay provisions do not apply to certain broadcasting personnel in Connecticut, Pennsylvania, and Vermont. In Connecticut[54] and Pennsylvania[55] minimum wage and overtime pay provisions do not apply to any person employed as an announcer, news editor, or chief engineer by a radio or television station. In Vermont minimum wage and overtime pay provisions do not apply to:

> Those employees of small market broadcasting stations referred to in section 13(b) (9) of the Federal Fair Labor Standards Act to whom the overtime provisions of the Federal Fair Labor Standards Act do not apply, but shall apply to all other employees of such businesses.[56]

Illegal Activities

The broadcasting of lottery information[57] and obscene language[58] are expressly prohibited by federal statutes in the United State Code. Nevertheless, Maine[59] and Wisconsin[60] have enacted similar statutes concerning the broadcasting of lotteries in their states, and Georgia,[61] North Carolina,[62] Washington,[63] and Wyoming[64] have statutes covering the broadcasting of obscenities, and ten other state legislatures have enacted laws that deal with the transmission of gambling information by broadcast. Indiana,[65] Tennessee,[66] and Texas[67] have enacted such statutes which, in general, make it unlawful to transmit information <u>prior</u> to the occurrence of any race, game, contest, or event on which gambling may be conducted, but do not forbid the transmission of information concerning the <u>results</u> of any such event.[68] Indeed, statutes in California,[69] Massachusetts,[70] and Michigan[71] construe the broadcasting of results of such gambling events as "news." Interestingly, Nevada accords a similar statutory construction for gambling events published by "newspapers of general circulation," but not for gambling events broadcast by radio or television.[72]

In Florida[73] and Louisiana,[74] the state racing commission may, by rule, permit the immediate transmission by broadcast of any pertinent information concerning "not more than two feature races each week." The 1970 Louisiana statute is an almost verbatim copy of the Florida statute, enacted in 1959.

Statutes in New York stipulate that the off-track pari-mutuel betting commission shall not make any broadcast of any horse race available for viewing or hearing in the public area of any facility where bets may be placed.[75] All radio broadcasting rights in the state of Washington in connection with horse racing meets are reserved to the state and the state racing commission shall lease or license same only to the highest bidder.[76] Furthermore, and perhaps more interesting, is the fact that all income derived from the exercise of such rights "shall be paid into the state treasury and credited to the old age pension fund."[77]

Miscellaneous Topics

The following group of state statutes deals with several miscellaneous topics from the use of fireworks to the promotion of poetry day by the broadcaster. Since California has enacted more of these statutes than any other single state, I will discuss all of the California laws first.

Every television studio in California that uses destructive devices in the conduct of its business, must obtain a permit (valid for a period of one year only) from the Chief of the Bureau of Criminal Identification and Investigation.[78] This permit is issued upon satisfactory showing by the television studio that a good cause exists for the issuance of said permit.[79] California's State Fire Marshal may adopt reasonable regulations providing for the granting of licenses and permits for the use of pyrotechnics by television special effects personnel.[80] Similar statutes in New York do not prohibit the use, storage, transportation, or sale for use "of fireworks in the preparation for or in connection with television broadcasts."[81]

Persons in California employed to render cosmetological services in the radio and television industry are exempt from the statutory provisions that stipulate various licensing requirements applicable to those engaged in the practice of cosmetology.[82] California law permits the posting against trespassing and loitering of property which consists of "plant, structures or facilities used for . . . radiobroadcasting."[83] For the purposes of unemployment insurance laws in California, the definition of "employment" includes "any service in an artistic or literary capacity performed by an individual" in the radio or television industry.[84] Other insurance laws in California indemnify the producer of any television production against loss by interruption, postponement, or cancellation of such production due to death, accidental injury, or sickness of performers or directors involved.[85] Florida's casualty insurance laws include similar provisions covering producers' indemnity insurance.[86]

The remaining state statutes covering miscellaneous business topics will be discussed on a state-by-state basis, since there is no pattern to the content of the laws. In both Maryland[87] and New York,[88] corporations operating radio broadcasting stations may restrict or limit the transferability to and ownership by aliens of shares of their stock. Another Maryland statute stipulates that no charitable organization may solicit contributions "by means of broadcast" over any radio or television station in the state, unless prior to such broadcast, the charitable organization has filed with the broadcasting station a certificate stating that the required information form has been filed with the Maryland Secretary of State.[89] Also, "the radio or television station shall not be required to make any other or further verification of such filing.[90]

A Tennessee statute, which states that standard time shall be observed in all parts of the state, as fixed by the U.S. Department of Transportation, also stipulates that no broadcasting station doing business in Tennessee shall "operate on, announce, employ, display, maintain or use any other standard of time than standard time as prescribed by this section."[91] A statute enacted by the Mississippi state legislature makes it unlawful for any person to bomb a radio station.[92]

Organizations defined as subversive in Louisiana are required by statutory law to attach to their registration statements written transcripts of any radio or television broadcast disseminated by the registering organization.[93] Michigan includes in its legal definition of "foreign agency" any "publishing enterprise, radio station, and/or similar institution for influencing public opinion . . . which has originated" with organizations defined as subversive in the law or, "who have come under the control of organizations serving the objects of a foreign power."[94] Michigan also has an early (1927) statute that regulates radio broadcasting originating within the state and prohibits interference in radio reception caused by simultaneous broadcasting.[95] Similarly, the director of regulatory agencies in Hawaii may employ an inspector "for the purpose of inspection of radio interferences and matters related thereto."[96]

The Department of Corrections in Illinois may allow a prisoner to appear on radio and television programs where the purpose is to obtain an understanding of the results, causes, and prevention of crime and criminality.[97]

Finally, the state of Maine designates October 15 as Poetry Day, and radio and television stations are encouraged to give recognition to the poets "who have helped or are helping to make Maine famous in the field of poetry throughout the world."[98]

FOOTNOTES

[1]47 U.S.C.A. Sec. 307(a) (1962).

[2]Several textbooks deal with the business of broadcasting. For example, see Ward L. Quaal and Leo A. Martin, _Broadcast Management_ (New York: Hastings House, 1968); J. Leonard Reinsch and Elmo Ellis, _Radio Station Management_ (New York: Harper & Row, 1960); and Yale Roe, ed., _Television Station Management_ (New York: Hastings House, 1964).

[3]_Del_. _Code_ _Ann_. tit. 30, Sec. 2301 (Cum. Supp. 1970).

[4]_Ariz_. _Rev_. _Stat_. _Ann_. Sec. 42-1371 (Supp. 1971).

[5]_Ibid_.

[6]_Hawaii_ _Rev_. _Stat_. Sec. 237-13(4) (1968).

[7]_Wash_. _Rev_. _Code_ _Ann_. Sec. 82.04.280 (Supp. 1971).

[8]_W_. _Va_. _Code_ _Ann_. Sec. 11-13-2g (Supp. 1971).

[9]_Me_. _Rev_. _Stat_. _Ann_. tit. 36, Sec. 1752 (Supp. 1972).

[10]_Community Telecasting Service_ v. _Johnson_, Me., 220 A.2d 500 (1966).

[11]_Ibid_.

[12]_Ibid_.

[13]Broadcasting and other mass media are businesses. As such, they are not immune from taxation placed upon other business enterprises, as long as such taxation falls with a more or less even hand upon the media as upon other businesses. However, discriminatory or punitive taxation raises some intriguing questions as to whether such taxation is an unconstitutional abridgement of the First and Fourteenth Amendments. For an interesting discussion of the issues involved, see Harold L. Nelson and Dwight L. Teeter, Jr., *Law of Mass Communications* (Mineola: The Foundation Press, Inc., 1969), pp. 512-519.

[14]*Del. Code Ann.* tit. 30, Sec. 2301 (Cum. Supp. 1970).

[15]*Ariz. Rev. Stat. Ann.* Sec. 42-1371 (Supp. 1971).

[16]*Wash. Rev. Code Ann.* Sec. 82.04.280 (Supp. 1971).

[17]*Hawaii Rev. Stat.* Sec. 237-13(4) (1968).

[18]*W. Va. Code Ann.* Sec. 11-13-2g (Supp. 1971).

[19]*Tex. Rev. Civ. Stat. Ann.* art. 7150 (Vernon's Supp. 1971).

[20]*Ind. Ann. Stat.* Sec. 64-1802 (IC 6-1-44-2) (repl. 1961).

[21]*Md. Ann. Code* art. 81, Sec. 12B (repl. 1969).

[22]*Fla. Stat. Ann.* Sec. 212.08 (Supp. 1972).

[23]*Miss. Code Ann.* Sec. 10146-04(g) (Supp. 1971).

[24]*Va. Code Ann.* Sec. 58-441.6 (repl. 1969).

[25]*S.C. Code Ann.* Sec. 65-1404 (26) (27) (Supp. 1971).

[26]*Ibid.*, (27).

[27]*Hawaii Rev. Stat.* Sec. 237-23(15) (1968).

[28]*N.Y. Tax Law* Sec. 1105 (McKinney Supp. 1971).

[29]*Mich. Comp. Laws Ann.* Sec. 205.94 (Supp. 1972).

[30]*Ibid.*, Sec. 205.54a.

[31]*Okla. Stat. Ann.* tit. 68, Sec. 2420 (1966).

[32]Tex. Rev. Civ. Stat. Ann. art. 179c (Vernon's 1969).

[33]Cal. Rev. & Tax. Code Sec. 24971 (West 1970).

[34]Ariz. Rev. Stat. Ann. Sec. 43-152(m) (Supp. 1971).

[35]Md. Ann. Code art. 100, Sec. 11(a) (Supp. 1971).

[36]Cal. Labor Code Sec. 1395 (West 1971).

[37]Fla. Stat. Ann. Sec. 450.132 (1966).

[38]Md. Ann. Code art. 100, Sec. 11(a) (Supp. 1971).

[39]Fla. Stat. Ann. Sec. 450.132(3) (1966).

[40]Md. Ann. Code art. 100, Sec. 11(a) (Supp. 1971).

[41]Mass. Gen. Laws Ann. ch. 149, Sec. 60 (1971).

[42]N.Y. Educ. Law Sec. 3229 (McKinney Supp. 1971).

[43]Ibid.

[44]Wis. Stat. Ann. Sec. 103.78 (1957).

[45]Ibid.

[46]Me. Rev. Stat. Ann. tit. 17, Sec. 3204 (Supp. 1972).

[47]Mass. Gen. Laws Ann. ch. 136, Sec. 6 (Supp. 1972).

[48]Miss. Code Ann. Sections 2369-04, 2370 (Supp. 1971).

[49]S.C. Code Ann. Sec. 64-2.1 (Supp. 1971).

[50]Ala. Code tit. 30, Sec. 3 (Cum. Supp. 1969).

[51]Colo. Rev. Stat. Ann. Sec. 78-1-3 (Supp. 1967).

[52]Fla. Stat. Ann. Sec. 40.08 (1961).

[53]Okla. Stat. Ann. tit. 38, Sec. 28 (Supp. 1971).

[54]Conn. Gen. Stat. Ann. Sec. 31-76i (Supp. 1971).

[55] Pa. Stat. Ann. tit. 43, Sec. 333.105 (Supp. 1971).

[56] Vt. Stat. Ann. tit. 21, Sec. 384 (Supp. 1971).

[57] 18 U.S.C.A. Sec. 1304 (1966).

[58] 18 U.S.C.A. Sec. 1464 (1966).

[59] Me. Rev. Stat. Ann. tit. 17, Sec. 1814 (1964).

[60] Wis. Stat. Ann. Const. art. 4, Sec. 24 (Supp. 1971).

[61] Ga. Code Ann. Sec. 26-2105 (1971).

[62] N.C. Gen. Stat. Sec. 14-190.1 et seq. (Supp. 1971).

[63] Wash. Rev. Code Ann. Sec. 9.68.010 et seq. (Supp. 1971).

[64] Wyo. Stat. Ann. Sec. 6-105.1 to 6-105.4 (Supp. 1971).

[65] Ind. Ann. Stat. Sec. 10-2333(IC 35-25-1-5) (repl. 1956).

[66] Tenn. Code Ann. Sections 39-2033(6), 39-2035 (Supp. 1971).

[67] Tex. Penal Code Ann. art. 652a (Vernon's 1952).

[68] Ind. Ann. Stat. Sec. 10-2333 (IC 35-25-1-5) (repl. 1956).

[69] Cal. Penal Code Sec. 337i (West 1970).

[70] Mass. Gen. Laws Ann. ch. 271, Sec. 31A (1970).

[71] Mich. Comp. Laws Ann. Sec. 750.305a (1968).

[72] Nev. Rev. Stat. Sec. 465.090 (1969).

[73] Fla. Stat. Ann. Sec. 550.35 (1962).

[74] La. Rev. Stat. Ann. Sec. 4:171.1 (Supp. 1972).

[75] N.Y. Unconsol. Laws Sec. 8070 (McKinney Supp. 1971).

[76] Wash. Rev. Code Ann. Sec. 67.16.110 (1962).

[77] *Ibid.*

[78] *Cal. Penal Code* Sec. 12305 (West 1970).

[79] *Ibid.*

[80] *Cal. Health & Safety Code* Sec. 12555 (West 1964).

[81] *N.Y. Penal Law* Sec. 270.00 (McKinney 1967).

[82] *Cal. Bus. & Prof. Code* Sec. 7320 et seq. (West 1964).

[83] *Cal. Penal Code* Sec. 554 (West Supp. 1972).

[84] *Cal. Un. Ins. Code* Sec. 601.5 (West Supp. 1972).

[85] *Cal. Ins. Code* Sec. 120 (West 1972).

[86] *Fla. Stat. Ann.* Sec. 624.605 (Supp. 1972).

[87] *Md. Ann. Code* art. 23, Sec. 29 (repl. 1966).

[88] *N.Y. Gen. Corp. Law.* Sec. 14 (McKinney Supp. 1971).

[89] *Md. Ann. Code* art. 41, Sec. 103B (repl. 1971).

[90] *Ibid.*

[91] *Tenn. Code Ann.* Sec. 4-113 (repl. 1971).

[92] *Miss. Code Ann.* Sec. 2143 (1957).

[93] *La. Rev. Stat. Ann.* Sec. 14:362 (Supp. 1972).

[94] *Mich. Comp. Laws Ann.* Sec. 14.201 et seq. (1967).

[95] *Mich. Comp. Laws Ann.* Sec. 484.301 et seq. (1967).

[96] *Hawaii Rev. Stat.* Sec. 269-4 (1968).

[97] *Ill. Ann. Stat.* ch. 108, Sec. 131 (Smith-Hurd Supp. 1972).

[98] *Me. Rev. Stat. Ann.* tit. 1, Sec. 112 (1964).

CHAPTER VII

SUMMARY AND CONCLUSIONS

This study was designed to answer one major question concerning broadcast regulation: What role are states playing in the regulation of commercial and educational radio and television broadcasting in the United States?

Broadcast regulation research has traditionally dealt only with federal laws and, consequently, regulatory controls of broadcasting at the state level have either been totally overlooked or, at best, treated minimally by the researcher.[1] Thus, there is a paucity of information about the aspects of broadcasting which are being regulated by the states, despite the fact that the legitimacy of state legislation relative to broadcasting has been clearly established by Congress and the courts. This study is an attempt to remedy this dearth of information; it is an examination of all state statutory laws that regulate various aspects of broadcasting.

Since the major question involves the statutory laws of the fifty states, the sources of data were the official compilations of all state laws. To ascertain what laws each state has on broadcasting, I examined all entries listed in each state's general indices and pocket supplements under three different headings: "Broadcasting," "Radio," and "Television." I departed from this procedure only when there was no entry for educational broadcasting. When this occurred, I checked each general index and its accompanying supplement under the heading "Education." This initial search of state laws was checked by repeating the entire process. The state statutes covered in this study were in force as of April 10, 1972.

As a further check on the accuracy of my search of the legal literature, I corresponded with the Attorney General in each state. In a letter to each I explained that I needed to know what laws his state has on broadcasting. I received forty responses. Of these forty, thirty-one were helpful in that they contained references to statutes, copies of the indices to the statutes, or copies of the statutes themselves. After examining all the statutes a second time, I checked my results against the information in these thirty-one responses. The accuracy of my search was substantiated to the extent that only three states sent references (one from each state) that my search had not uncovered.

The focus of this study is upon only those statutes that directly affect commercial and educational radio and television broadcasting. It does not deal with statutes which regulate areas which are, at most, tangential to the operation of a broadcasting station. The excluded statutes include those on CATV, booster or translator systems, subscription television, closed-circuit telecasts, amateur or shortwave radio, and statutes applicable to public utilities generally.

All indexed entries were systematically recorded and the applicable statutes read and examined to determine whether they were relevant to the study. Those that were relevant were examined as a group and a classification system was devised. The classification system developed from the fact that the statutes show that there are four major areas of regulation with which these state laws are concerned: 1) broadcasting and individual rights, 2) educational broadcasting, 3) advertising, and 4) business aspects of broadcasting.

Following the initial classification, the statutes were further divided within each of the four major areas into groups of statutory laws that regulate the same matter. Comparative examinations were then made of the related statutes from the different states comprising each group. These examinations focused upon the following: 1) uniformity in wording across states, 2) similarities/differences/inconsistencies in purpose or intent of the law, 3) unique or noteworthy statutory provisions, and 4) enactment dates. These examinations revealed patterns among the state statutes which in turn led to analyses of related federal legislation, relevant court decisions, and administrative-agency promulgations. Further examinations and analyses of the statutes were made in accordance with the questions detailed in Chapter I.

Results

The extent to which the fifty states are currently regulating various aspects of commercial and educational broadcasting is astounding in two respects. First, every state has enacted at least one statutory law governing some aspect of broadcasting; second, a total of eighty-six different aspects of broadcasting are regulated.

The most state legislative activity is in the area discussed in Chapter III, "Broadcasting and Individual Rights." Only two states, Kansas and Vermont, have no statutes covering any of the twenty-nine topics discussed in Chapter III.[2] Statutes on broadcasting and individual rights cover three major issues: 1) defamation/libel/slander, 2) the right of privacy, and 3) the right to know. Most state legislative activity has focused on matters pertaining to defamation/libel/slander, particularly on protecting the broadcaster from liability for defamatory statements broadcast by candidates for public office. It was found that these statutes were enacted during a period in which broadcasters were faced with a liability dilemma as the result of the *Sorensen* rule and the subsequent, controversial FCC *Port Huron* decision.

These state statutes remain in force today, although they have been superseded by the 1959 U.S. Supreme Court decision in *Farmers Union*. Since the development of *Farmers Union* provides an insightful look at the interaction of federal and state legislation in the same area, it was discussed fully in Chapter III. Included among the statutes discussed in relationship to the "Right of Privacy" were those on privileged sources of information, Canon 35, and juvenile hearings. Statutes pertaining to the broadcasting of public meetings and hearings were included in the discussion of legislation affecting the "Right to Know."

The second most active area of state legislation is that related to advertising. Forty-three states have enacted statutory laws governing one or more of the thirty-one advertising matters discussed in Chapter V. These statutes fall into two major categories: *general* legal controls over fraudulent advertising, deceptive trade, and consumer fraud practices; and *specific* legal controls over foods, drugs, and cosmetics, political advertising, and various commodities such as insurance, loans, and real estate. It was found that initial legislation on the regulation of fraudulent advertising was enacted at the state level, subsequent to the 1911 publication of the *Printers' Ink* model statute. Also, an interesting trend away from regulating advertisers and towards providing statutory protection for disseminators of advertisements was discerned. To illustrate this pattern, the development of and interaction between federal and state advertising legislation were traced over the same period of years.

Statutes on educational broadcasting and related matters were discussed in Chapter IV. The major finding was that state legislative activity followed certain federal legislation on educational broadcasting. It was also found that the most fruitful method of examining these statutes necessitated grouping the thirty-five states according to two criteria. The first criterion is whether an existing state agency or a specially created one is given control of educational broadcasting within the state. Several states have placed such development in the hands of state departments of education or universities, while other states have created special educational broadcasting commissions. The second criterion is the relative amount of control that state legislatures give to these agencies as evidenced by the delegated powers set forth in the statutes. Some agencies are given merely an advisory role, others primarily coordinating, while still others are given a broad legal mandate to supervise and control all aspects of educational broadcasting within the state. Various statutory restrictions which some states have imposed on educational broadcasters were discussed. Special attention was directed to examining an apparent statutory conflict between the "public interest" standard of the Communications Act and the no-editorializing provision of Section 399 of the 1967 Public Broadcasting Act.

Of the four major areas of regulation, business aspects of broadcasting have received the least legislative attention by the states. Indeed, nineteen states have nothing to say about any one of the twenty-five topics discussed in Chapter VI. Statutes enacted by the thirty-one "active" states are diverse in matters regulated; they include laws affecting personnel, programming, general operations, and fiscal practices of broadcasting. Taxes receive more statutory attention than any other single aspect of the business of broadcasting and their regulation by the states is discussed fully in Chapter VI.

Although the states collectively regulate a wide range of matters, eighty-six in all, only three are regulated by one-half or more of the states. The most frequently regulated across all fifty states is educational broadcasting. In Chapter IV I discussed the various kinds of state commissions and agencies established in the thirty-five states that have enacted legislation in the area. The next most frequently occurring type of legislation among the states deals with immunization of the owner, licensee, or operator of a broadcasting station from liability for damages for any defamatory statement made by candidates for public office. Thirty-one states have enacted such legislation. Similar legislation, enacted by twenty-six states, immunizes the owner, licensee, or operator from liability for defamatory statements made by persons who are neither candidates for public office nor licensees or owners of broadcasting stations. Nearly one-half of the states (23) have enacted fraudulent advertising statutes.

California has been the most active state in enacting statutory laws on the various aspects of commercial and educational broadcasting discussed in this study. Such activity on the part of the California State Legislature is indicated by the following. First, by having statutes on twenty-five of the eighty-six aspects covered in this study, California outranks all states in the total number of matters regulated. The second and third most active states, New York and Illinois, have enacted laws on seventeen and fifteen aspects respectively. Second, although a few states have been quite active in <u>one</u> major area of regulation,[3] California has been very active in all four areas of regulation. Indeed, California leads all states in the number of aspects regulated in two major areas ("Broadcasting and Individual Rights" and "The Business of Broadcasting") and shares the lead with New York and Illinois in the total number of statutes enacted relative to "Broadcasting and Advertising."

Discussion

The preceding section summarized the findings relative to this study's major question concerning broadcast regulation. This study also sought to answer various subsidiary--though important--questions concerning broadcast legislation at the state level. In this section I will deal with these questions in the order in which they were detailed in Chapter I.

1) How general (across states) is each regulation? There was great heterogeneity among the fifty states in the eighty-six aspects of broadcasting which are regulated. The greatest homogeneity among the states was found in the statutes that immunize broadcasters from liability for defamatory statements made by political speakers, that grant statutory protection to the reporter-informant confidential relationship, that provide for the establishment of some sort of educational broadcasting commission, and that protect broadcasters from liability for disseminating fraudulent, deceptive, or misleading advertisements. Even in these areas, though, only 70 per cent of the states regulated any one facet of broadcasting (educational broadcasting). On the other hand, the majority of the eighty-six aspects of broadcasting covered by statutory laws were enacted by no more than one or two states. Such heterogeneity apparently reflects the sovereignty of each of the several states to determine for itself the kinds of

statutes to be enacted or the kinds of activities to be regulated in a given state. Undoubtedly, it also reflects the different kinds of pressure groups operating within each state. The fact that the states have acted in such a heterogeneous fashion might account for the lack of regional patterns and contiguous states effects to be discussed in questions four and five.

2) Are there redundancies in the law? Although some federal court decisions have superseded existing state statutes in some areas, in general, the states have not enacted legislation on broadcast matters which are currently covered by federal laws. Rather, the characteristic pattern across all states has been one of enacting statutory laws to complement and supplement federal statutes or federal court decisions. Moreover, some states have sought to enumerate certain illegal practices which are prohibited by a more ambiguous federal law. This was especially evident among the states which sought to clarify the Federal Trade Commission Act's general proscription of "deceptive acts or practices."

3) Are there inconsistencies among states on statutes that cover the same topics? There were no clear inconsistencies found among the state statutes regulating the same topics. However, in those areas where states have acted to implement and supplement existing federal legislation, state statutes apparently reflect differing

philosophies of the role of state government or the rights to be accorded broadcasters. For example, statutes on educational broadcasting are so disparate in wording, purpose, and length, that no two states can be said to share the same view of noncommercial broadcasting and its relationship to state control. However, where states have acted to protect broadcasters threatened by an inconsistency in federal law, there is almost no variation in the wording or purpose of the state statutes. Such was the case when federal law enjoined broadcasters from censoring the speeches of political office seekers without providing them immunity from civil and criminal defamation actions in state courts. In the instances where states have acted in areas not covered at all by federal law, such as in the protection of the reporter-informant confidential relationship, the state statutes again reflect differing views of the broadcaster's rights.

4) Do some state statutes reflect regional patterns? Examination of the state statutes covered in this study revealed no consistent regional pattern. Few state broadcast regulations are more prevalent in one area of the country than another.

5) Are there signs of contiguous states effects? Although no consistent regional patterns were found in the order in which states legislate, a few signs of contiguous states effects were evident. Broadcast legislation often

follows the customary practice of a state looking to its neighbors for examples of applicable legislation when it decides to act on a particular matter.

6) Do some states appear to play the role of "leader" or "innovator" in broadcast legislation? As discussed in the preceding section on "Results," it was found that California, New York, and Illinois ranked first, second, and third respectively in the total number of broadcast matters regulated. It is interesting to note that these same three states achieved identical ranking in a 1970 legislative evaluation study which examined how well the fifty state legislatures measure up to minimum standards of legislative capability.[4]

7) Do some states have a law in certain areas that could serve as a model for other states to adopt? Various statutory provisions were discussed in this study as model legislation. They dealt with the right of privacy, advertising, the right to know, and educational broadcasting. These provisions will be discussed further below.

Those states considering the enactment of "shield laws" designed to protect the confidential relationships between broadcast reporters and their informants should examine the provisions contained in the various statutes granting qualified and absolute privileges enacted by the fourteen states discussed in Chapter III. It should be noted, however, that none of the state statutes currently in force grants absolute protection from compulsory disclosure of both the identities of informants and the information received from them.[5] If a state should decide to grant such absolute statutory protection, the U.S. Supreme Court has indicated that this would be a valid exercise of state legislative activity.[6] In noting that no statutory privilege has been provided by federal statute, and that a number of states have provided newsmen with statutory privileges of varying breadth,[7] the U.S. Supreme Court in *Branzburg* stated:

> There is also merit in leaving state legislatures free, within First Amendment limits, to fashion their own standards in light of the conditions and problems with respect to the relations between law enforcement officials and press in their own areas. It goes without saying, of course, that we are powerless to erect any bar to state courts responding in their own way and construing their own constitutions so as to recognize a newsman's privilege, either qualified or absolute.[8]

Another area in which several states have acted is that of advertising. As discussed in Chapter V, eleven states have adopted *qualified* statutory exemptions designed to relieve the broadcaster from liability for disseminating a fraudulent advertisement. These exemptions are qualified to the extent that if such an advertisement is broadcast "in good faith and without knowledge" of its false, deceptive, or misleading character, then the broadcaster is not liable. Statutes in these eleven states could serve as model legislation for other states considering acting in this area. Adoption of such qualified exemptions appears to be in the best possible "public interest" since the unscrupulous broadcaster could abuse privileges inherent in an absolute statutory exemption. The public or consumer interest would be served because such a qualified exemption apparently makes the broadcaster partially responsible for the advertising carried by his station. Thus, the broadcaster would have a stake in protecting consumer interests in the United States.

As discussed in Chapter III, both the public's right to know and the "accountability" of state legislatures are well-served in the five states that have enacted statutes allowing broadcast coverage at public meetings. These statutes could serve as model legislation for other states considering acting in this area. States wishing to immunize the broadcaster from liability for prosecution for a fair and true report of such public meetings (including judicial and legislative proceedings) should examine the provisions contained in the Montana[9] and Utah[10] laws.

The Oklahoma statutes governing noncommercial broadcasting were discussed in Chapter IV as being both comprehensive and detailed and worthy of adoption by other states. However, it was noted in that chapter that the states differ widely in their conception of the purpose and role of educational broadcasting and, therefore, might not wish to adopt the entire group of Oklahoma statutes.

Some provisions, however, consistent with the way other states view noncommercial broadcasting, might serve as models.

The unique provision in the Florida statute[11] that provides for the use of educational television for discussion between political candidates in order to help reduce excessive campaign costs appears to be worth the consideration of other states. The legislative development and background of this provision were fully discussed in Chapter IV.

In addition to the answers found to the seven subsidiary questions of this study, a clear picture of the relationship between state and federal activity in the area of broadcasting emerged. In general federal action has acted as a catalyst for state regulatory activity. The latter generally follows the lead of federal legislation, judicial decisions, and/or administrative-agency promulgations. This pattern is consistent across the four major areas of state regulation discussed in this study. It is especially evident in educational broadcasting, the statutes on broadcast defamation, and the statutes on advertising, especially in laws governing food and drug activities.

Implications For Future Research

This study has confirmed the fact that the field of broadcast regulation has not been completely preempted by federal law. The states have a right to regulate certain aspects of broadcasting. Indeed, the results of this study show that the states have exercised this right to cover a surprisingly wide range of aspects.

However, no attempt was made in this study to assess the impact or effectiveness of state statutory laws. Such a study needed to wait upon the discovery and analysis of precisely what laws have been enacted. Hopefully, by providing a working knowledge of state statutory laws, the results reported in this work will provoke future research on state broadcast legislation.

It seems to me that the next logical step is to determine the enforceability of these state statutes. How effective are they in regulating what they are designed to regulate? How often are the statutes tested in court? Are certain kinds of statutes or statutes which regulate certain kinds of activities more effective than others?

Future research might also examine whether there are any manifest differences in the broadcasting service in those states which have more active legislatures and more comprehensive legislation in this field.[12] Another fruitful research area, largely empirical, would be to measure broadcasters' awareness and knowledge of these state statutes, and the role which these state laws play in the composite day-to-day broadcasting picture.

The resurgence of regulatory activity by state legislatures along with recent court decisions can only serve to enlarge the role which state regulation of broadcasting will play in the future. Hopefully, the results of the present study and those from future research will provide the broadcast scholar and practitioner with the necessary means to deal effectively with state legislatures in providing the best possible environment for the development and continued growth of broadcasting.

FOOTNOTES

[1]For example, see Kenneth S. Devol, ed., _Mass Media and the Supreme Court_ (New York: Hastings House, Publishers, Inc., 1971); Walter B. Emery, _Broadcasting and Government: Responsibilities and Regulations_ (East Lansing: Michigan State University Press, 1971); Donald M. Gillmor and Jerome A. Barron, _Mass Communication Law: Cases and Comment_ (St. Paul: West Publishing Co., 1969); and Harold L. Nelson and Dwight L. Teeter, Jr., _Law of Mass Communications_ (Mineola: The Foundation Press, Inc., 1969).

[2]Kansas and Vermont _may_ have some general statutes which cover these matters, but even if they do their relevance to broadcasting is probably not as clear and specific as in the other forty-eight states. Such statutes (if they exist) are indexed in Kansas' and Vermont's statutory compilations under headings other than those which I examined. As a result, by following the research method outlined in Chapter II, one would not be able to retrieve them. These same comments apply to those states which my research has shown to be deficient in broadcast legislation in other areas.

[3]Nevada and Utah in "Broadcasting and Individual Rights"; Illinois, Massachusetts, and New York in "Broadcasting and Advertising"; and Florida and New York in "The Business of Broadcasting."

[4]The overall rankings arrived at in the study were based upon a consolidation of factors under five major category groupings: functional, accountable, informed, independent, and representative. See John Burns, _The Sometime Governments: A Critical Study of the 50 American Legislatures_ (New York: Bantam Books, Inc., 1971), p. 48.

[5]For an interesting discussion of whether the First Amendment should guarantee a broad right to keep the identities of informants and their communications confidential, see Note, "Reporters and Their Sources: The Constitutional Right to a Confidential Relationship," 80 _Yale Law Journal_ 317 (1970).

[6]*Branzburg* v. *Hayes*, 40 LW 5025 (1972).

[7]*Ibid*., p. 5032.

[8]*Ibid*., p. 5037.

[9]*Mont*. *Rev*. *Codes* *Ann*. Sec. 94-2807 (repl. 1969).

[10]*Utah* *Code* *Ann*. Sec. 76-40-6 (Supp. 1971).

[11]*Fla*. *Stat*. *Ann*. Sec. 229.805(5a) (Supp. 1972).

[12]An empirical problem that would require measurement of programming diversity as well as content analyses in sample markets.

TABLE 1

State Statutory Compilations Used In This Thesis

Code of Alabama Recompiled
Alaska Statutes Annotated
Arizona Revised Statutes Annotated
Arkansas Statutes Annotated
West's Annotated California Codes

Colorado Revised Statutes Annotated
Connecticut General Statutes Annotated
Delaware Code Annotated
Florida Statutes Annotated
Code of Georgia Annotated

Hawaii Revised Statutes
Idaho Code Annotated
Smith-Hurd Illinois Annotated Statutes
Burns Annotated Indiana Statutes
Iowa Code Annotated

Kansas Statutes Annotated
Baldwin's Kentucky Revised Statutes Annotated
West's Louisiana Revised Statutes Annotated
Maine Revised Statutes Annotated
Annotated Code of Maryland

Massachusetts General Laws Annotated
Michigan Compiled Laws Annotated
Minnesota Statutes Annotated
Mississippi Code Annotated
Missouri Revised Statutes

Revised Codes of Montana Annotated
Revised Statutes of Nebraska
Nevada Revised Statutes
New Hampshire Revised Statutes Annotated
New Jersey Statutes Annotated

New Mexico Statutes Annotated
McKinney's Consolidated Laws of New York Annotated
General Statutes of North Carolina
North Dakota Century Code Annotated
Page's Ohio Revised Code Annotated

TABLE 1 (cont'd.)

Oklahoma Statutes Annotated
Oregon Revised Statutes
Purdon's Pennsylvania Statutes Annotated
General Laws of Rhode Island Annotated
Code of Laws of South Carolina Annotated

South Dakota Compiled Laws Annotated
Tennessee Code Annotated
Vernon's Annotated Revised Statutes of Texas
Utah Code Annotated
Vermont Statutes Annotated

Code of Virginia Annotated
Revised Code of Washington Annotated
West Virginia Code Annotated
West's Wisconsin Statutes Annotated
Wyoming Statutes Annotated

TABLE 2

State Statutes On Broadcasting And Individual Rights

Defamation/Libel/Slander

Political Candidates

Ariz. Rev. Stat. Ann. Sec. 12-652(B) (1956)
Ark. Stat. Ann. Sec. 3-1108 (Supp. 1971)
Cal. Civ. Code Sec. 48.5(3) (West 1954)
Colo. Rev. Stat. Ann. Sec. 41-2-6 (1963)
Conn. Gen. Stat. Ann. Sec. 52-239 (1960)

Ga. Code Ann. Sec. 105-713 (1968)
Hawaii Rev. Stat. Sec. 751-11 (1968)
Idaho Code Sec. 6-701 (Supp. 1971)
Ky. Rev. Stat. Ann. Sec. 411.062 (Baldwin's 1969)
La. Rev. Stat. Ann. Sec. 45:1352 (1951)

Me. Rev. Stat. Ann. tit. 17, Sec. 2203 (1964)
Md. Ann. Code art. 75, Sec. 6 (repl. 1969)
Mich. Comp. Laws Ann. Sec. 484.332 (1967)
Miss. Code Ann. Sec. 1059.5(2) (1957)
Mo. Rev. Stat. Sec. 537.105 (1969)

Mont. Rev. Codes Ann. Sec. 64-205 (repl. 2d 1970)
Neb. Rev. Stat. Sec. 86-602 (1971)
Nev. Rev. Stat. Sec. 41.360 (1969)
N.H. Rev. Stat. Ann. Sec. 507-A:2 (repl. 1968)
N.J. Stat. Ann. Sec. 2A:43-3 (Supp. 1971)

N.Y. Civ. Rights Law Sec. 75 (McKinney Supp. 1971)
Ohio Rev. Code Ann. Sec. 2739.03(A) (Page 1954)
Okla. Stat. Ann. tit. 12, Sec. 1447.2 (1961)
Ore. Rev. Stat. Sec. 30.150(2) (1971)
S.C. Code Ann. Sec. 23-7 (1962)

Tenn. Code Ann. Sec. 23-2607 (Supp. 1971)
Utah Code Ann. Sec. 45-2-5 (repl. 1970)
Va. Code Ann. Sec. 8-632.1 (repl. 1957)
W. Va. Code Ann. Sec. 55-7-14 (1966)
Wis. Stat. Ann. Sec. 895.052 (1966)

TABLE 2 (cont'd.)

Wyo. Stat. Ann. Sec. 1-873 (1957)

Non-Candidates, Non-Licensees

Ariz. Rev. Stat. Ann. Sec. 12-652(A) (1956)
Cal. Civ. Code Sec. 48-5(1) (West 1954)
Colo. Rev. Stat. Ann. Sec. 41-2-6 (1963)
Fla. Stat. Ann. Sec. 770.04 (1964)
Ga. Code Ann. Sec. 105-712 (1968)

Iowa Code Ann. Sec. 659.5 (1950)
Ky. Rev. Stat. Ann. Sec. 411.062 (Baldwin's 1969)
La. Rev. Stat. Ann. Sections 14:50, 45:1351 (1951)
Mich. Comp. Laws Ann. Sec. 484.331 (1967)
Minn. Stat. Ann. Sec. 544.043 (Supp. 1971)

Miss. Code Ann. Sec. 1059.5(1) (1957)
Neb. Rev. Stat. Sec. 86-601 (1971)
Nev. Rev. Stat. Sec. 41.340 (1969)
N.H. Rev. Stat. Ann. Sec. 507-A:1 (repl. 1968)
N.M. Stat. Ann. Sec. 40-27-35 (repl. 1964)

N.C. Gen. Stat. Sec. 99-5 (repl. 1965)
N.D. Cent. Code Sec. 14-02-09 (repl. 1971)
Ohio Rev. Code Ann. Sec. 2739.03(B) (Page 1954)
Okla. Stat. Ann. tit. 12, Sec. 1447.1 (1961)
Ore. Rev. Stat. Sec. 30.150(1) (1971)

S.D. Compiled Laws Ann. Sec. 20-11-6 (1967)
Tenn. Code Ann. Sec. 23-2606 (Supp. 1971)
Tex. Rev. Civ. Stat. Ann. art. 5433a (Vernon's 1958)
Va. Code Ann. Sec. 8-632.1 (repl. 1957)
W. Va. Code Ann. Sec. 55-7-14 (1966)

Wyo. Stat. Ann. Sec. 1-872 (1957)

Uniform Single Publication Act

Ariz. Rev. Stat. Ann. Sec. 12-651 (1956)
Cal. Civ. Code Sec. 3425.1 et seq. (West 1970)
Idaho Code Sec. 6-702 (Supp. 1971)
Ill. Ann. Stat. ch. 126, Sections 11-15 (Smith-Hurd 1967)
N.M. Stat. Ann. Sections 40-27-30 to 34 (repl. 1964)

N.D. Cent. Code Sec. 14-02-10 (repl. 1971)
Pa. Stat. Ann. tit. 12, Sec. 2090.1 (1967)

TABLE 2 (cont'd.)

Fair Reports Of Governmental Proceedings

Mont. Rev. Codes Ann. Sec. 94-2807 (repl. 1969)
Utah Code Ann. Sec. 76-40-6 (Supp. 1971)

Furnishing Libelous Statements

N.J. Stat. Ann. Sec. 2A:120-1 (1969)
Pa. Stat. Ann. tit. 18, Sec. 4413.1 (1963)

Miscellaneous

SCRIPTS

Fla. Stat. Ann. Sec. 770.03 (1964)
Idaho Code Sec. 6-707 (Supp. 1971)
Mont. Rev. Codes Ann. Sec. 64-206 (repl. 2d 1970)
Utah Code Ann. Sec. 45-2-6 (repl. 1970)
Wash. Rev. Code Ann. Sec. 19.64.010 (1961)

NETWORK BROADCASTS

Cal. Civ. Code Sec. 48.5(2) (West 1954)
Idaho Code Sec. 6-709 (Supp. 1971)
N.H. Rev. Stat. Ann. Sec. 507-A:3 (repl. 1968)
Utah Code Ann. Sec. 45-2-8 (repl. 1970)

COMPENSATORY DAMAGES

Ariz. Rev. Stat. Ann. Sec. 12-653.02 (Supp. 1971)
Ga. Code Ann. Sec. 105-714 (1968)
Idaho Code Sec. 6-712 (Supp. 1971)
Ind. Ann. Stat. Sec. 2-518 (IC 34-4-14-1) (repl. 1967)
Iowa Code Ann. Sec. 659.2 (Supp. 1972)

La. Rev. Stat. Ann. Sec. 45:1353 (1951)
Miss. Code Ann. Sec. 1059.7(2) (Supp. 1971)
Mont. Rev. Codes Ann. Sec. 64-207.1 (Supp. 1971)
Neb. Rev. Stat. Sec. 86-603 (1971)
Nev. Rev. Stat. Sec. 41.336 (1969)

TABLE 2 (cont'd.)

N.C. Gen. Stat. Sec. 99-2 (Supp. 1971)
Ohio Rev. Code Ann. Sec. 2739.03 (Page 1954)
Okla. Stat. Ann. tit. 12, Sec. 1447.5 (1961)
Ore. Rev. Stat. Sec. 30.160 (1971)
Wyo. Stat. Ann. Sec. 1-874 (1957)

GENERAL LIBEL

Me. Rev. Stat. Ann. tit. 17, Sec. 2203 (1964)
Mass. Gen. Laws Ann. ch. 231, Sec. 91A (1959)
Pa. Stat. Ann. tit. 12, Sec. 1585 (Supp. 1971)

SLANDER OF THE DEAD

N.D. Cent. Code Sec. 12-28-15 (1960)

CRIMINAL DEFAMATION

Ill. Ann. Stat. ch. 38, Sections 27-1, 27-2 (Smith-Hurd 1970)

The Right Of Privacy

Privileged Sources

Ala. Code tit. 7, Sec. 370 (1960)
Ariz. Rev. Stat. Ann. Sec. 12-2237 (Supp. 1971)
Ark. Stat. Ann. Sec. 43-917 (repl. 1964)
Cal. Evid. Code Sec. 1070 (West Supp. 1972)
Ill. Ann. Stat. ch. 51, Sec. 111 et seq. (Smith-Hurd Supp. 1972)

Ind. Ann. Stat. Sec. 2-1733 (IC 34-3-5-1) (repl. 1968)
Ky. Rev. Stat. Ann. Sec. 421.100 (Baldwin's 1969)
La. Rev. Stat. Ann. Sec. 45:1451 et seq. (Supp. 1972)
Md. Ann. Code art. 35, Sec. 2 (repl. 1971)
Mont. Rev. Codes Ann. Sec. 93-601-2 (repl. 1964)

Nev. Rev. Stat. Sec. 48.087 (1969)
Ohio Rev. Code Ann. Sec. 2739.04 (Page Supp. 1971)
Pa. Stat. Ann. tit. 28, Sec. 330 (1958)
R.I. Gen. Laws Ann. Sec. 9-19.1-1 et seq. (Supp. 1971)

TABLE 2 (cont'd.)

Canon 35

Alaska Civ. R. 46(i) (1963)
Del. Code Ann. Super. Cr. Rule 53 (1971)
Nev. Rev. Stat. Sections 1.220, 178.604 (1971)
N.M. Stat. Ann. Sections 21-1-1(90), 21-2-1(27) (repl. 1970)
N.Y. Judiciary Law, Judic. Appendix Rule 20.5 (McKinney Supp. 1971)

Pa. Stat. Ann., R.C.P. (tit. 12), Rule 223 (1967)
Wyo. Stat. Ann., W.R. Cr. P., Rule 50 (1971)

Miscellaneous

WITNESSES

Ill. Ann. Stat. ch. 51, Sec. 57 (Smith-Hurd 1966)
N.Y. Civ. Rights Law Sec. 52 (McKinney Supp. 1971)

JUVENILE HEARINGS

Iowa Code Ann. Sec. 232.27 (1969)
Nevada Senate Bill NO. 365 (approved March 1971)
N.H. Rev. Stat. Ann. Sec. 169:27 (Supp. 1971)
Utah Code Ann. Sec. 55-10-94 (Supp. 1971)

EAVESDROPPING

Ill. Ann. Stat. ch. 38, Sec. 14-1 et seq. (Smith-Hurd 1972)
Wash. Rev. Code Ann. Sec. 9.73.030 et seq. (Supp. 1971)

CRIME COMMISSIONS

Cal. Penal Code Sec. 6028.1 (West 1970)

VOTERS

Mass. Gen. Laws Ann. ch. 54, Sec. 76 (Supp. 1972)

TABLE 2 (cont'd.)

NAME OR LIKENESS

Fla. *Stat*. *Ann*. Sections 540.08 to .10 (Supp. 1972)

CHILD MOLESTER ACT

Fla. *Stat*. *Ann*. Sec. 801.221 (Supp. 1972)

BASTARDY ACT

Fla. *Stat*. *Ann*. Sec. 742.09 (Supp. 1972)

The Right To Know

Supplementary Broadcasts

Del. *Code* *Ann*. tit. 6, Sec. 3801 et seq. (Supp. 1970)
Idaho *Code* Sections 60-110 to 112 (Supp. 1971)
Ky. *Rev*. *Stat*. *Ann*. Sec. 424.195 (Baldwin's Supp. 1971)
Mont. *Rev*. *Codes* *Ann*. Sections 19-201 to 203 (repl. 1967)
Ore. *Rev*. *Stat*. Sections 193.310 et seq., 255.510 (1971)

Utah *Code* *Ann*. Sec. 45-1-3 et seq. (Supp. 1971)
Wash. *Rev*. *Code* *Ann*. Sec. 29.27.072 (Supp. 1971)
Wash. *Rev*. *Code* *Ann*. Sections 65.16.130 to 150 (1966)

Public Meetings

Cal. *Gov't* *Code* Sections 6090, 6091 (West 1966)
Conn. *Gen*. *Stat*. *Ann*. Sec. 1-21a (1969)
Ind. *Ann*. *Stat*. Sections 57-607 to 609 (IC 4-22-3-1 to 4-22-3-3) (repl. 1961)
Me. *Rev*. *Stat*. *Ann*. tit. 1, Sec. 403 (Supp. 1972)
Neb. *Rev*. *Stat*. Sec. 84-1401 et seq. (1971)

Miscellaneous

LOBBYISTS

Ill. *Ann*. *Stat*. ch. 63, Sec. 171 et seq. (Smith-Hurd Supp. 1972)
N.J. *Stat*. *Ann*. Sec. 52:13C-1 et seq. (1970)
N.C. *Gen*. *Stat*. Sec. 120-48 et seq. (repl. 1964)
Tenn. *Code* *Ann*. Sec. 39-5001 et seq. (Supp. 1971)

TABLE 2 (cont'd.)

LEGISLATURES

Conn. Gen. Stat. Ann. Sec. 2-51 (1969)

ELECTIONS

Ind. Ann. Stat. Sections 29-3302 (IC 3-1-6-2), 29-5024 (IC 3-1-23-24) (Supp. 1971)

DISASTER AREAS

Cal. Penal Code Sec. 409.5 (West 1970)

EXECUTIONS

Okla. Stat. Ann. tit. 22, Sec. 1015 (1958)

JUVENILE HEARINGS--FELONY

Iowa Code Ann. Sec. 232.27 (1969)
Nevada Senate Bill NO. 365 (approved March 1971)
N.H. Rev. Stat. Ann. Sec. 169:27 (Supp. 1971)
Utah Code Ann. Sec. 55-10-94 (Supp. 1971)

TABLE 3

State Statutes On Educational Broadcasting

Specially Created Commissions

Take-Over Commissions

ALABAMA
Ala. Code tit. 52, Sec. 627 et seq. (1960)
ALASKA
Alaska Stat. Sec. 14.58.010 et seq. (1971)
ARKANSAS
Ark. Stat. Ann. Sec. 80-3901 et seq. (Supp. 1971)
IOWA
Iowa Code Ann. Sections 8A.1 et seq., 19B.3 (Supp. 1972)
House File 738, 64th General Assembly (1971)
KENTUCKY
Ky. Rev. Stat. Ann. Sec. 168.010 et seq. (Baldwin's Supp. 1971)
MARYLAND
Md. Ann. Code art. 77, Sections 29, 80, 161 (repl. 1969)
MASSACHUSETTS
Mass. Gen. Laws Ann. ch. 6, Sec. 158 (Supp. 1972)
Mass. Gen. Laws Ann. ch. 71, Sec. 13F (Supp. 1972)
Mass. Gen. Laws Ann. ch. 71, Sections 13G,H,I (1969)
Mass. Gen. Laws Ann. ch. 69, Sec. 1, note (1969)
MISSISSIPPI
Miss. Code Ann. Sections 6411-15, 8946-101 et seq. (Supp. 1971)
NEBRASKA
Neb. Rev. Stat. Sections 72-718.03, 79-2101 et seq. (1971)
NEW JERSEY
N.J. Stat. Ann. Sections 48:23-1 et seq., 54:4-3.6a (Supp. 1971)
OKLAHOMA
Okla. Stat. Ann. tit. 70, Sections 23-101 et seq., 2166, 2167 (Supp. 1971)
PENNSYLVANIA
Pa. Stat. Ann. tit. 71, Sec. 1188.1 et seq. (Supp. 1971)
Pa. Stat. Ann. tit. 24, Sections 5-523,5-525, 9-964(7) (Supp. 1971)
Pa. Stat. Ann. tit. 24, Sec. 2822(3) (1962)

TABLE 3 (cont'd.)

SOUTH CAROLINA

S.C. Code Ann. Sections 21-60.3 to 21-60.5, 21-412.2 (Supp. 1971)

S.C. Code Ann. Sections 21-60, 21-60.1,.2 (1962)

SOUTH DAKOTA

Senate Bill 127 (1972)

S.D. Compiled Laws Ann. Sections 13-47-1, 13-47-6, 13-47-18 to 13-47-23 (Supp. 1971)

S.D. Compiled Laws Ann. Sections 13-47-2 to 13-47-5, 13-47-7 to 13-47-17 (1967)

WISCONSIN

Wis. Stat. Ann. Sections 15.643, 36.063, 39.09, .11, .13 (Supp. 1971)

Wis. Stat. Ann. Sec. 36.33 (1966)

Coordinating Commissions

LOUISIANA

La. Rev. Stat. Ann. Sec. 17:2501 et seq. (Supp. 1972)

La. Rev. Stat. Ann. Sections 25:701-703 (1969)

NEVADA

Nev. Rev. Stat. Sec. 398.010 et seq. (1971)

OHIO

Ohio Rev. Code Ann. Sec. 5705.05 (Page Supp. 1971)

Ohio Rev. Code Ann. Sec. 3353.01 et seq. (Page Supp. 1970)

UTAH

Utah Code Ann. Sec. 53-42-1 et seq. (repl. 1970)

VIRGINIA

Va. Code Ann. Sections 22-332, 334, 344, 344.1, .2, 29-11 (Supp. 1971)

Va. Code Ann. Sections 22-331, 333, 335 to 343 (repl. 1969)

Va. Code Ann. Sec. 15.1-23 (repl. 1964)

WEST VIRGINIA

W. Va. Code Ann. Sec. 10-5-2 (Supp. 1971)

W. Va. Code Ann. Sections 10-5-1, 10-5-3 to 10-5-5 (repl. 1969)

Advisory Commissions

NORTH DAKOTA

N.D. Cent. Code Sections 15-11-27, 15-47-36, 15-65-01 et seq. (repl. 1971)

WASHINGTON

Wash. Rev. Code Ann. Sec. 28A.91.010 et seq. (1970)

TABLE 3 (cont'd.)

Existing State Agencies

State Boards Of Education

DELAWARE
Del. Code Ann. tit. 14, Sections 132-134 (Cum. Supp. 1970)
FLORIDA
Fla. Stat. Ann. Sections 229.805, 230.59 et seq., 235.40 (Supp. 1972)
GEORGIA
Ga. Code Ann. Sections 32-408.1 et seq., 32-621 (1969)
OREGON
Ore. Rev. Stat. Sec. 354.010 et seq. (1971)
RHODE ISLAND
R.I. Gen. Laws Ann. Sec. 16-28-1 et seq. (Reenactment of 1969)
TENNESSEE
Tenn. Code Ann. Sections 49-3801 to 49-3807 (Supp. 1971)
Tenn. Code Ann. Sec. 49-3808 (repl. 1966)

Universities

MAINE
Me. Rev. Stat. Ann. tit. 13, Sec. 932 (Supp. 1972)
Me. Rev. Stat. Ann. tit. 20, Sections 2601, 2603, 2605 (Supp. 1972)
Me. Rev. Stat. Ann. tit. 36, Sec. 1760 (Supp. 1972)
Me. Rev. Stat. Ann. tit. 20, Sections 2602, 2604 (1964)
NEW MEXICO
N.M. Stat. Ann. Sections 73-26-34, 35 (Supp. 1971)
VERMONT
Vt. Stat. Ann. tit. 16, Sec. 2801 et seq. (1968)

Board Of Regents

NEW YORK
N.Y. Educ. Law Sections 213, 236, 414-a (McKinney 1969)

TABLE 3 (cont'd.)

Department Of General Services

CALIFORNIA

Cal. Gov't Code Sections 14716 et seq., 26155 (West Supp. 1972)

Cal. Educ. Code Sections 893.20, .21 (West Supp. 1972)

Cal. Rev. & Tax. Code Sections 214, 215.5, 225.5 (West 1970)

Superintendent Of Public Instruction

MONTANA

Mont. Rev. Codes Ann. Sections 75-5710, 5711 (2d repl. 1971)

TABLE 4

State Statutes On Broadcasting And Advertising

General Legal Controls

Fraudulent Advertising--Printers' Ink

Ark. Stat. Ann. Sec. 41-1961 et seq. (Supp. 1971)
Cal. Bus. & Prof. Code Sec. 17500 et seq. (West 1964)
Conn. Gen. Stat. Ann. Sec. 42-115a (Supp. 1971)
Ga. Code Ann. Sec. 106-503 (1968)
Hawaii Rev. Stat. Sections 747-14, 747-15 (1968)

Ill. Ann. Stat. ch. 121 1/2, Sec. 157.21a et seq. (Smith-Hurd Supp. 1972)
La. Rev. Stat. Ann. Sec. 51:411 (1965)
Me. Rev. Stat. Ann. tit. 17, Sec. 1620 (1964)
Md. Ann. Code art. 27, Sec. 198 (repl. 1971)
Mass. Gen. Laws Ann. ch. 266, Sec. 91B (1970)

Mich. Comp. Laws Ann. Sections 750.33, 750.33a (1968)
Minn. Stat. Ann. Sec. 325.905 (Supp. 1971)
Mo. Rev. Stat. Sec. 561.665 (1969)
Nev. Rev. Stat. Sec. 207.170 (1971)
N.Y. Gen. Bus. Law Sec. 396 (McKinney 1968)

Pa. Stat. Ann. tit. 18, Sec. 4857 (1963)
Tenn. Code Ann. Sec. 39-1945 (Supp. 1971)
Utah Code Ann. Sec. 76-4-1 (1953)
Va. Code Ann. Sec. 59.1-44 et seq. (repl. 1968)
W. Va. Code Ann. Sec. 61-3-38 (1966)

Wis. Stat. Ann. Sec. 100.18(2)(8)(9)(10)(11) (Supp. 1971)
Wis. Stat. Ann. Sec. 100.18(1)(3)(4)(5)(6)(7) (1957)

TABLE 4 (cont'd.)

Fraudulent Advertising--Non-Printers' Ink

Ind. Ann. Stat. Sec. 10-3037 (IC 35-17-5-10) (Supp. 1971)
Mich. Comp. Laws Ann. Sec. 445.801 et seq. (1967)
N.M. Stat. Ann. Sections 49-12-2, 49-12-5.1 to 49-12-5.3 (Supp. 1971)
N.M. Stat. Ann. Sections 49-12-1, 49-12-3 to 49-12-7 (repl. 1966)
N.Y. Gen. Bus. Law Sec. 350 et seq. (McKinney 1968)

Uniform Deceptive Trade Practices Act

Conn. Gen. Stat. Ann. Sec. 42-115c et seq. (Supp. 1971)
Del. Code Ann. tit. 6, Sec. 2531 et seq. (Supp. 1970)
Fla. Stat. Ann. Sec. 817.69 et seq. (Supp. 1972)
Ill. Ann. Stat. ch. 121 1/2, Sec. 311 et seq. (Smith-Hurd Supp. 1972)
Neb. Rev. Stat. Sec. 87-301 et seq. (1971)

Consumer Fraud

Ariz. Rev. Stat. Ann. Sec. 44-1521 et seq. (1967)
Ark. Stat. Ann. Sec. 70-901 et seq (Supp. 1971)
Cal. Civ. Code Sec. 1750 et seq. (West Supp. 1972)
Del. Code Ann. tit. 6, Sec. 2511 et seq. (Supp. 1970)
Ill. Ann. Stat. ch. 121 1/2, Sec. 261 et seq. (Smith-Hurd Supp. 1972)

Iowa Code Ann. Sec. 713.24 (Supp. 1972)
Kan. Stat. Ann. Sec. 50-601 et seq. (Supp. 1968)
Md. Ann. Code art. 83, Sec. 21 (repl. 1969)
Minn. Stat. Ann. Sec. 325.79 (Supp. 1971)
Mo. Rev. Stat. Sec. 407.010 et seq. (1969)

N.J. Stat. Ann. Sec. 56:8-1 et seq. (Supp. 1971)
N.Y. Gen. Bus. Law Sec. 349 (McKinney Supp. 1971)
N.C. Gen. Stat. Sec. 75-1.1 (Supp. 1971)
N.D. Cent. Code Sec. 51-15-01 et seq. (Supp. 1971)
Tex. Rev. Civ. Stat. Ann. art. 5069-10.01 et seq. (Vernon's 1971)

Vt. Stat. Ann. tit. 9, Sec. 2451 et seq. (1970-1971)

TABLE 4 (cont'd.)

Specific Legal Controls

Foods, Drugs, Cosmetics

Alaska Stat. Sec. 17.20.290 et seq. (1962)
Ariz. Rev. Stat. Ann. Sec. 36-914 (Supp. 1971)
Ark. Stat. Ann. Sec. 82-1101 et seq. (repl. 1960)
Cal. Health & Safety Code Sec. 26467 (West Supp. 1972)
Conn. Gen. Stat. Ann. Sec. 19-215 (1969)

Ill. Ann. Stat. ch. 56 1/2, Sec. 505 (Smith-Hurd Supp. 1972)
Ind. Ann. Stat. Sec. 35-3120 (IC 16-1-28-20) (repl. 1969)
Kan. Stat. Ann. Sec. 65-659 (1964)
Me. Rev. Stat. Ann. tit. 22, Sec. 2166 (1964)
Md. Ann. Code art. 43, Sec. 187D (Supp. 1971)

N.M. Stat. Ann. Sec. 54-6-30 (Supp. 1971)
N.M. Stat. Ann. Sec. 54-1-5 (repl. 1962)
N.Y. Agric. & Mkts. Law Sec. 202-a (McKinney 1954)
Ohio Rev. Code Ann. Sec. 3715.54 (Page 1971)
Ore. Rev. Stat. Sec. 616.275 (1971)

R.I. Gen. Laws Ann. Sec. 21-31-1 et seq. (Reenactment of 1968)
Va. Code Ann. Sec. 3.1-390 (repl. 1966)
Wash. Rev. Code Ann. Sec. 69.04.090 (1962)

Political Advertising

Alaska Stat. Sec. 15.55.040 (1971)
Ariz. Rev. Stat. Ann. Sec. 19-128 (Supp. 1971)
Cal. Elections Code Sec. 11700 et seq. (West Supp. 1972)
Ky. Rev. Stat. Ann. Sec. 123.095 (Baldwin's Supp. 1971)
Miss. Code Ann. Sections 3176, 3178 (1957)

Ohio Rev. Code Ann. Sec. 3599.09 (Page Supp. 1970)
Tex. Election Code Ann. art. 14.10(b) (Vernon's Supp. 1971)
Tex. Election Code Ann. art. 14.10(a)(c)(d) (Vernon's 1967)
Va. Code Ann. Sec. 24.1-259 (Supp. 1971)
Wis. Stat. Ann. Sections 12.14, 12.15 (1967)

TABLE 4 (cont'd.)

Insurance--Domestic

Fla. Stat. Ann. Sections 626.954, 631.65 (Supp. 1972)
Hawaii Rev. Stat. Sections 431-150, 431-643 (1968)
Ill. Ann. Stat. ch. 73, Sec. 761 (Smith-Hurd 1965)
Kan. Stat. Ann. Sec. 40-2404 (1964)
La. Rev. Stat. Ann. Sec. 22:1214 (1959)

Mass. Gen. Laws Ann. ch. 176D, Sec. 1 et seq. (1958)
Minn. Stat. Ann. Sec. 72A.20 et seq. (1968)
Nev. Rev. Stat. Sec. 686.420 (1969)
Pa. Stat. Ann. tit. 40, Sec. 1152 (Supp. 1971)
Wis. Stat. Ann. Sec. 207.01 et seq. (1957)

Insurance--Foreign

Hawaii Rev. Stat. Sec. 421-327 (1968)
La. Rev. Stat. Ann. Sec. 22:1231 et seq. (Supp. 1972)
La. Rev. Stat. Ann. Sec. 22:1523 (1959)
Mass. Gen. Laws Ann. ch. 175, Sections 160A, 160B (1958)
Minn. Stat. Ann. Sec. 72A.33 et seq. (1968)

Nev. Rev. Stat. Sec. 686.480 (1967)
Pa. Stat. Ann. tit. 18, Sec. 4689 (1963)
Wis. Stat. Ann. Sec. 207.04 (Supp. 1971)

Loans

Ariz. Rev. Stat. Ann. Sec. 6-535 (Supp. 1971)
Cal. Fin. Code Sec. 18617 (West Supp. 1972)
Cal. Fin. Code Sections 5050 et seq., 12300 et seq., 22000 et seq., 24410 (West 1968)
Conn. Gen. Stat. Ann. Sec. 36-376 (1969)
Del. Code Ann. tit. 5, Sec. 3127 (Supp. 1970)

Hawaii Rev. Stat. Sec. 476-35 (1968)
Kan. Stat. Ann. Sec. 16-418 (1964)
Md. Ann. Code art. 58A, Sec. 15 (repl. 1972)
Minn. Stat. Ann. Sec. 56.12 (1970)
Miss. Code Ann. Sec. 5591-05 (Supp. 1971)

TABLE 4 (cont'd.)

Neb. Rev. Stat. Sec. 69-1214 (1971)
Okla. Stat. Ann. tit. 14A, Sec. 2-313 (Supp. 1971)
Ore. Rev. Stat. Sec. 697.790 (1971)
Utah Code Ann. Sec. 58-30-13 (repl. 1963)
Wis. Stat. Ann. Sec. 138.09 (Supp. 1971)

Wis. Stat. Ann. Sec. 214.16 (1957)

Professions

DENTISTS/DENTAL HYGIENISTS

Ill. Ann. Stat. ch. 91, Sec. 62 (Smith-Hurd Supp. 1972)
Iowa Code Ann. Sec. 153.32 (Supp. 1972)
Kan. Stat. Ann. Sec. 65-1423 (Supp. 1968)
Md. Ann. Code art. 32, Sec. 18 (repl. 1971)
Mass. Gen. Laws Ann. ch. 112, Sections 52A, 52B, 52C (1971)

N.Y. Gen. Bus. Law Sec. 396-c (McKinney 1968)
Okla. Stat. Ann. tit. 59, Sections 328.28, 328.29 (1971)
Pa. Stat. Ann. tit. 63, Sec. 122 (1968)
Tex. Penal Code Ann. art. 752a,b (Vernon's 1961)

LAWYERS

Cal. Bus. & Prof. Code Sec. 6076, rule 18 (West 1962)

PSYCHOLOGISTS

Wash. Rev. Code Ann. Sec. 18.83.120 (Supp. 1971)

OPTOMETRISTS

Hawaii Rev. Stat. Sec. 459-9 (1968)
Mass. Gen. Laws Ann. ch. 112, Sec. 73A (1971)

ELECTROLOGISTS

Mass. Gen. Laws Ann. ch. 112, Sec. 87KKK (1971)

TABLE 4 (cont'd.)

DRUGGISTS

Conn. Gen. Stat. Ann. Sec. 19-241 (1969)

BARBERS

Neb. Rev. Stat. Sec. 71-223.02 (1971)

Real Estate

Cal. Bus. & Prof. Code Sec. 11022 (West 1964)
Conn. Gen. Stat. Ann. Sec. 20-329k (Supp. 1971)
Fla. Stat. Ann. Sec. 478.011 et seq. (Supp. 1972)
Fla. Stat. Ann. Sec. 475.47 (1965)
N.Y. Real Prop. Law Sec. 337-b(3) (McKinney Supp. 1971)

Miscellaneous

SECURITIES

Ill. Ann. Stat. ch 121 1/2, Sec. 137.9 (Smith-Hurd 1960)
Nev. Rev. Stat. Sec. 90.140 (1971)
Nev. Rev. Stat. Sec. 90.210 (1969)
N.J. Stat. Ann. Sec. 49:3-33 (1970)
Ore. Rev. Stat. Sec. 59.345 (1971)

Tex. Rev. Civ. Stat. Ann. art. 581-22 (Vernon's 1964)

LIQUOR

Me. Rev. Stat. Ann. tit. 28, Sec. 5 (1964)
N.H. Rev. Stat. Ann. Sec. 175:10 (Supp. 1971)
N.J. Stat. Ann. Sec. 33:1-39 (Supp. 1971)
Tex. Penal Code Ann. art. 667-24a(2) (Vernon's Supp. 1971)
Tex. Penal Code Ann. art. 667-24a(1)(3)(4) (Vernon's 1952)

CONTRACEPTIVES

Ariz. Rev. Stat. Ann. Sec. 13-537 (Supp. 1971)
Del. Code Ann. tit. 16, Sec. 2502 (1953)
Utah Code Ann. Sec. 58-19-10 (repl. 1963)

TABLE 4 (cont'd.)

RELIGIOUS DISCRIMINATION

Fla. _Stat_. _Ann_. Sec. 871.04 (1965)
_Va_. _Code_ _Ann_. Sec. 57-2.1 (repl. 1969)

ADOPTION

Cal. _Civ_. _Code_ Sec. 224p (West Supp. 1972)
Nev. _Rev_. _Stat_. Sec. 127.310 (1967)

BINGO

_N.J_. _Stat_. _Ann_. Sec. 5:8-36 (1959)
_N.Y_. _Gen_. _Munic_. _Law_ Sec. 490 (McKinney Supp. 1971)

RAFFLES

_N.J_. _Stat_. _Ann_. Sec. 5:8-63 (1959)

IMPORTED GOODS

Mass. _Gen_. _Laws_ _Ann_. ch. 94, Sec. 277B (1972)

CEMETERY LOTS

_N.Y_. _Gen_. _Bus_. _Law_ Sec. 451 (McKinney 1968)

CITY BONDS

Ore. _Rev_. _Stat_. Sections 287.002, 552.660 (1971)

ABORTIONS

Ill. _Ann_. _Stat_. ch. 38, Sections 23-2, 23-3 (Smith-Hurd 1970)

AGRICULTURAL PRODUCTS

_Va_. _Code_ _Ann_. Sec. 59.1-54 (repl. 1968)

TABLE 4 (cont'd.)

POULTRY AND EGGS

Neb. *Rev*. *Stat*. Sections 81-2,164.01, .02, .03 (1971)

APPLES

Me. *Rev*. *Stat*. *Ann*. tit. 7, Sec. 536 (1964)

TABLE 5

State Statutes On The Business Of Broadcasting

Taxes

Taxable Items

Ariz. Rev. Stat. Ann. Sec. 42-1371 (Supp. 1971)
Del. Code Ann. tit. 30, Sec. 2301 (Cum. Supp. 1970)
Hawaii Rev. Stat. Sec. 237-13(4) (1968)
Me. Rev. Stat. Ann. tit. 36, Sec. 1752 (Supp. 1972)
Wash. Rev. Code Ann. Sec. 82.04.280 (Supp. 1971)

W. Va. Code Ann. Sec. 11-13-2g (Supp. 1971)

Tax Exemptions

Fla. Stat. Ann. Sec. 212.08 (Supp. 1972)
Hawaii Rev. Stat. Sec. 237-23(15) (1968)
Ind. Ann. Stat. Sec. 64-1802 (IC 6-1-44-2) (repl. 1961)
Md. Ann. Code art. 81, Sec. 12B (repl. 1969)
Mich. Comp. Laws Ann. Sections 205.54a, 205.94 (Supp. 1972)

Miss. Code Ann. Sec. 10146-04(g) (Supp. 1971)
N.Y. Tax Law Sec. 1105 (McKinney Supp. 1971)
S.C. Code Ann. Sec. 65-1404 (26) (27) (Supp. 1971)
Tex. Rev. Civ. Stat. Ann. art. 7150 (Vernon's Supp. 1971)
Va. Code Ann. Sec. 58-441.6 (repl. 1969)

Miscellaneous Tax Statutes

PERSONAL PROPERTY

Okla. Stat. Ann. tit. 68, Sec. 2420 (1966)

BROADCASTING RECORDS

Tex. Rev. Civ. Stat. Ann. art. 179c (Vernon's 1969)

TABLE 5 (cont'd.)

SALE OF BROADCASTING PROPERTY OR STOCK

Ariz. Rev. Stat. Ann. Sec. 43-152(m) (Supp. 1971)
Cal. Rev. & Tax. Code Sec. 24971 (West 1970)

Employment Practices

Employment of Minors

Cal. Labor Code Sections 1394.5, 1395 (West 1971)
Fla. Stat. Ann. Sections 450.081, 450.132 (1966)
Md. Ann. Code art. 100, Sec. 11(a) (Supp. 1971)
Md. Ann. Code art. 100, Sec. 11(b) (repl. 1964)
Mass. Gen. Laws Ann. ch. 149, Sections 60, 66 (1971)

N.Y. Educ. Law Sec. 3229 (McKinney Supp. 1971)
N.Y. Educ. Law Sec. 3230 (McKinney 1970)
Wis. Stat. Ann. Sec. 103.78 (1957)

Sundays

Me. Rev. Stat. Ann. tit. 17, Sec. 3204 (Supp. 1972)
Mass. Gen. Laws Ann. ch. 136, Sec. 6 (Supp. 1972)
Miss. Code Ann. Sections 2369-04, 2370 (Supp. 1971)
S.C. Code Ann. Sec. 64-2.1 (Supp. 1971)

Jury Duty Exemptions

Ala. Code tit. 30, Sec. 3 (Cum. Supp. 1969)
Colo. Rev. Stat. Ann. Sec. 78-1-3 (Supp. 1967)
Fla. Stat. Ann. Sec. 40.08 (1961)
Okla. Stat. Ann. tit. 38, Sec. 28 (Supp. 1971)

Wages

Conn. Gen. Stat. Ann. Sec. 31-76i (Supp. 1971)
Pa. Stat. Ann. tit. 43, Sec. 333.105 (Supp. 1971)
Vt. Stat. Ann. tit. 21, Sec. 384 (Supp. 1971)

TABLE 5 (cont'd.)

Illegal Activities

Lotteries

Me. Rev. Stat. Ann. tit. 17, Sec. 1814 (1964)
Wis. Stat. Ann. Const. art. 4, Sec. 24 (Supp. 1971)

Obscenities

Ga. Code Ann. Sec. 26-2105 (1971)
N.C. Gen. Stat. Sec. 14-190.1 et seq. (Supp. 1971)
Wash. Rev. Code Ann. Sec. 9.68.010 et seq. (Supp. 1971)
Wyo. Stat. Ann. Sec. 6-105.1 to 6-105.4 (Supp. 1971)

Gambling Information

Cal. Bus. & Prof. Code Sec. 19664 (West Supp. 1972)
Cal. Penal Code Sec. 337i (West 1970)
Fla. Stat. Ann. Sec. 550.35 (1962)
Ind. Ann. Stat. Sec. 10-2333 (IC 35-25-1-5) (repl. 1956)
La. Rev. Stat. Ann. Sec. 4:171.1 (Supp. 1972)

Mass. Gen. Laws Ann. ch. 271, Sec. 31A (1970)
Mich. Comp. Laws Ann. Sec. 750.305a (1968)
Nev. Rev. Stat. Sections 463.430, 465.090 (1969)
N.Y. Unconsol. Laws Sec. 8070 (McKinney Supp. 1971)
Tenn. Code Ann. Sections 39-2033(6), 39-2035 (Supp. 1971)

Tex. Penal Code Ann. art. 652a (Vernon's 1952)
Wash. Rev. Code Ann. Sec. 67.16.110 (1962)

Miscellaneous Topics

DESTRUCTIVE DEVICES--PYROTECHNICS

Cal. Penal Code Sec. 12305 (West 1970)
Cal. Health & Safety Code Sec. 12555 (West 1964)
N.Y. Penal Law Sec. 270.00 (McKinney 1967)

COSMETOLOGY

Cal. Bus. & Prof. Code Sec. 7320 et seq. (West 1964)

TABLE 5 (cont'd.)

POSTING AGAINST TRESPASSING

Cal. _Penal_ _Code_ Sec. 554 (West Supp. 1972)

UNEMPLOYMENT INSURANCE

Cal. _Un_. _Ins_. _Code_ Sec. 601.5 (West Supp. 1972)

PRODUCERS INDEMNITY INSURANCE

Cal. _Ins_. _Code_ Sec. 120 (West 1972)
Fla. _Stat_. _Ann_. Sec. 624.605 (Supp. 1972)

STOCK/ALIENS

_Md_. _Ann_. _Code_ art. 23, Sec. 29 (repl. 1966)
_N.Y_. _Gen_. _Corp_. _Law_. Sec. 14 (McKinney Supp. 1971)

CHARITABLE ORGANIZATIONS

_Md_. _Ann_. _Code_ art. 41, Sec. 103B (repl. 1971)

STANDARD TIME

Tenn. _Code_ _Ann_. Sec. 4-113 (repl. 1971)

BOMBING

Miss. _Code_ _Ann_. Sec. 2143 (1957)

SUBVERSIVE ORGANIZATIONS--FOREIGN AGENCIES

_La_. _Rev_. _Stat_. _Ann_. Sec. 14:362 (Supp. 1972)
Mich. _Comp_. _Laws_ _Ann_. Sec. 14.201 et seq. (1967)

INTERFERENCES

Hawaii _Rev_. _Stat_. Sec. 269-4 (1968)
Mich. _Comp_. _Laws_ _Ann_. Sec. 750.510 (1968)
Mich. _Comp_. _Laws_ _Ann_. Sec. 484.301 et seq. (1967)

TABLE 5 (cont'd.)

PRISONERS

Ill. Ann. Stat. ch. 108, Sec. 131 (Smith-Hurd Supp. 1972)

POETRY DAY

Me. Rev. Stat. Ann. tit. 1, Sec. 112 (1964)

BIBLIOGRAPHY

Books

Burns, John. *The Sometime Governments: A Critical Study of the 50 American Legislatures*. New York: Bantam Books, Inc., 1971.

Devol, Kenneth S., ed. *Mass Media and the Supreme Court*. New York: Hastings House, Publishers, Inc., 1971.

Emery, Walter B. *Broadcasting and Government: Responsibilities and Regulations*. East Lansing: Michigan State University Press, 1971.

Gillmor, Donald M., and Barron, Jerome A. *Mass Communication Law: Cases and Comment*. St. Paul: West Publishing Co., 1969.

Nelson, Harold L., and Teeter, Dwight L., Jr. *Law of Mass Communications*. Mineola: The Foundation Press, Inc., 1969.

Prosser, William L. *The Law of Torts*. 4th ed. St. Paul: West Publishing Co., 1971.

Quaal, Ward L., and Martin, Leo A. *Broadcast Management*. New York: Hastings House, Publishers, Inc., 1968.

Reinsch, J. Leonard, and Ellis, Elmo. *Radio Station Management*. New York: Harper & Row, 1960.

Roe, Yale., ed. *Television Station Management*. New York: Hastings House, Publishers, Inc., 1964.

Articles and Periodicals

Belstock, Lee J. "Free Press--Fair Trial--Cameras in the Courtroom." *University of Colorado Law Review*, XXXVIII (1966), 276-279.

Case Note. "Constitutional Law--Televising Criminal Trial of Widespread Public Interest Inherently Deprives Defendant of Due Process of Law." Fordham Law Review, XXXIV (1965), 329-336.

"CBS and CONGRESS: 'The Selling of the Pentagon' Papers." Educational Broadcasting Review, Special Issue (1971-1972).

"Developments in the Law--Deceptive Advertising." Harvard Law Review, LXXX (1967), 1005-1163.

Donnelly, R. C. "History of Defamation." Wisconsin Law Review, MCMIL (1949), 99-126.

Emery, Walter B. "Is There a Constitutional Flaw In the Public Broadcasting Act of 1967?" Educational Broadcasting Review, II (1968), 17-21.

Goldhill, Walter A. "Censorship of Political Broadcasts." Yale Law Journal, LVIII (1949), 787-795.

Kintner, Earl W. "Federal Trade Commission Regulation of Advertising." Michigan Law Review, LXIV (1966), 1269-1284.

MacIver, R. M. "The Role of the People." In Basic Issues of American Democracy. New York: Appleton-Century-Crofts, 1965. Pp. 13-18.

"Maine's Educational Television Network: Legal Difficulties." Maine Law Review, XXII (1970), 239-264.

Millstein, Ira M. "The Federal Trade Commission and False Advertising." Columbia Law Review, LXIV (1964), 439-499.

Payne, Gordon R. "ADMINISTRATIVE LAW: Libel Without Liability?" The Georgetown Law Journal, XXXVII (1949), 383-393.

Recent Cases. "Constitutional Law--Televising of Criminal Trials Held Violative of the Right to a Fair Trial." Vanderbilt Law Review, XVIII (1965), 2049-2055.

"Reporters and Their Sources: The Constitutional Right to a Confidential Relationship." Yale Law Journal, LXXX (1970), 317-371.

Romer, John Irving. "Legal Repression of Dishonest Advertising." Printers' Ink, November 16, 23, 30, 1911.

"The Supreme Court, 1958 Term." Harvard Law Review, LXXIII (1959), 233-240.

Toohey, Daniel W. "The Avoidance of Offense: Observations on the Matter of Broadcast Censorship." Saint Louis University Law Journal, XV (1970), 48-72.

Warden, Karl P. "Canon 35: Is There Room For Objectivity." Washburn Law Journal, IV (1965), 211-239.

Zuckman, Harvey L. "Censorship of Defamatory Political Broadcasts: The Port Huron Doctrine." New York University Law Review, XXXIV (1959), 127-140.

Court Cases

Alberty v. Federal Trade Commission, 182 F.2d 36 (D.C. Cir. 1950), cert. denied, 340 U.S. 818 (1950).

Allen B. Dumont Laboratories, Inc. v. Carroll, 184 F.2d 153 (1950).

Baltimore Radio Show, Inc. v. Maryland, cert. denied, 338 U.S. 912 (1950).

Branzburg v. Hayes, 40 LW 5025 (1972).

Branzburg v. Pound, Ky., 461 S.W. 2d 345 (1971).

California Democratic Council v. Arnebergh, 5 RR 2d 2073 (Cal. App. 1965).

Community Telecasting Service v. Johnson, Me., 220 A.2d 500 (1966).

Double-Eagle Lubricants, Inc. v. Texas, 248 F.Supp. 515 (N.D. Texas, 1965).

Estes v. Texas, 381 U.S. 532 (1965).

Farmers Educational & Cooperative Union v. WDAY, 89 N.W. 2d 102 (1958), 360 U.S. 525 (1959).

Federal Radio Commission v. Nelson Brothers, 289 U.S. 266 (1933).

Federal Trade Commission v. Raladam Co., 283 U.S. 643 (1931).

Federal Trade Commission v. Winsted Hosiery Company, 258 U.S. 483 (1922).

Florida Lime & Avocado Growers v. Paul, 373 U.S. 132 (1963).

General Electric Co. v. Federal Radio Commission, 31 F.(2d) 630 (App. D.C. 1929).

Head v. New Mexico Board of Examiners in Optometry, 374 U.S. 424 (1963).

Irvin v. Dowd, 366 U.S. 717 (1961).

Lipps v. State, 258 N.E. 2d 622 (1970).

Los Angeles Free Press, Inc. v. City of Los Angeles, 88 Cal. Rptr. 605, 9 C.A.3d 448 (1970).

McCaw v. Fase, 216 F.2d 700 (CA 9th, 1954).

McGoldrick v. Berwind-White Coal Mining Co., 309 U.S. 33 (1940).

Mosey Cafe, Inc. v. Licensing Board For the City of Boston, 154 N.E. 2d 585 (Mass. 1958).

Pacific Coast Dairy, Inc. v. Department of Agriculture of California, 318 U.S. 285 (1943).

Pulitzer Pub. Co. v. Federal Communications Commission, 94 F.2d 249 (1937).

R.C. Tway Coal Co. v. Glen, 12 F.Supp. 570 (1935).

Rideau v. Louisiana, 373 U.S. 723 (1963).

Sears, Roebuck & Co. v. Federal Trade Commission, 258 F. 307 (7th Cir. 1919).

Sheppard v. Maxwell, 384 U.S. 333 (1966).

Sorensen v. Wood, 123 Neb. 348, 243 N.W. 82 (1932), appeal dismissed 290 U.S. 599 (1933).

State of Maine v. University of Maine, Me., 266 A.2d 863 (1970).

State v. *Sheridan*, 248 Md. 320, 236 A.2d 18 (1967).

Tri-City Broadcasting Co. v. *Bowers*, 158 N.E. 2d 203 (1959).

United States v. *City of Chester*, 144 F.2d 415 (1944).

Whitehurst v. *Grimes*, 21 F.(2d) 787 (1927).

Other Works Cited

Code of Federal Regulations. 47 (1972), 73.503, 73.621.

Corpus Juris Secundum. 81 (1953), *States*, 871-872.

Federal Communications Commission Reports. 8 (1940), 333-341; 12 (1948), 1069-1084; 13 (1949), 1246-1270.

Federal Register. 16 (April 7, 1951), 3072-3090; 17 (May 2, 1952), 3905-4100.

Food Drug Cosmetic Law Reporter. All States. (1964, revised 1969), 10,101-10,125.

Pike and Fischer's *Radio Regulation Reporter*. Current Service Volumes, 53:503, 53:621; Opinion of the Attorney General of Louisiana, 14 RR 2050 (1956); Opinion of the Attorney General of Michigan, 12 RR 2d 2145 (1968); Opinion of the Attorney General of Missouri, 21 RR 2d 2114 (1971).

Radio Code. 17th ed. Washington, D.C.: Code Authority, National Association of Broadcasters, April 1972.

Television Code. 16th ed. Washington, D.C.: Code Authority, National Association of Broadcasters, April 1972.

United States Code Annotated. 15, Sections 41, 45 et seq., 52, 54(b), 55(a)(1), 1011 et seq. (1963); 18, Sections 1304, 1464 (1966); 21, Sec. 301 et seq. (1961); 47, Sections 151 et seq., 307(a) (1962), Sec. 390 et seq. (Supp. 1972).

U.S. Const. art. I, sec. 8(3).

United States Statutes At Large. 34 (1906), 768-772; 38 (1914), 717-724; 52 (1938), 111-117; 59 (1945), 33-34; 80 (1966), 1296-1302.

DISSERTATIONS IN BROADCASTING

An Arno Press Collection

Bailey Robert Lee. **An Examination of Prime Time Network Television Special Programs, 1948 to 1966.** *(Doctoral Thesis, University of Wisconsin, 1967)* 1979

Burke, John Edward. **An Historical-Analytical Study of the Legislative and Political Origins of the Public Broadcasting Act of 1967.** *(Doctoral Dissertation, The Ohio State University, 1971)* 1979

Foley, K. Sue. **The Political Blacklist in the Broadcast Industry:** The Decade of the 1950s. *(Doctoral Dissertation, The Ohio State University, 1972)* 1979

Hess, Gary Newton. **An Historical Study of the Du Mont Television Network.** *(Doctoral Dissertation, Northwestern University, 1960)* 1979

Howard, Herbert H. **Multiple Ownership in Television Broadcasting:** Historical Development and Selected Case Studies. *(Doctoral Dissertation, Ohio University, 1973)* 1979

Jameson, Kay Charles. **The Influence of the United States Court of Appeals for the District of Columbia on Federal Policy in Broadcast Regulation, 1929-1971.** *(Doctoral Dissertation, University of Southern California,1972)* 1979

Kirkley, Donald Howe, Jr. **A Descriptive Study of the Network Television Western During the Seasons 1955-56 to 1962-63.** *(Doctoral Dissertation, Ohio University, 1967)* 1979

Kittross, John Michael. **Television Frequency Allocation Policy in the United States.** *(Doctoral Dissertation, University of Illinois, 1960)* 1979

Larka, Robert. **Television's Private Eye:** An Examination of Twenty Years Programming of a Particular Genre, 1949 to 1969. *(Doctoral Dissertation, Ohio University, 1973)* 1979

Long, Stewart Louis. **The Development of the Television Network Oligopoly.** *(Doctoral Thesis, University of Illinois at Urbana-Champaign, 1974)* 1979

MacFarland, David T. **The Development of the Top 40 Radio Format.** *(Doctoral Thesis, University of Wisconsin, 1972)* 1979

McMahon, Robert Sears. **Federal Regulation of the Radio and Television Broadcast Industry in the United States, 1927-1959:** With Special Reference to the Establishment and Operation of Workable Administrative Standards. *(Doctoral Dissertation, The Ohio State University, 1959)* 1979

Muth, Thomas A. **State Interest in Cable Communications.** *(Doctoral Dissertation, The Ohio State University, 1973)* 1979

Pearce, Alan. **NBC News Division:** A Study of the Costs, the Revenues, and the Benefits of Broadcast News and **The Economics of Prime Time Access.** *(Doctoral Dissertation, Indiana University, 1972)* 1979

Pepper, Robert M. **The Formation of the Public Broadcasting Service.** *(Doctoral Dissertation, University of Wisconsin, 1975)* 1979

Pirsein, Robert William. **The Voice of America:** A History of the International Broadcasting Activities of the United States Government, 1940-1962. *(Doctoral Dissertation, Northwestern University, 1970)* 1979

Ripley, Joseph Marion, Jr. **The Practices and Policies Regarding Broadcasts of Opinions about Controversial Issues by Radio and Television Stations in the United States.** *(Doctoral Dissertation, The Ohio State University, 1961)* 1979

Robinson, Thomas Porter. **Radio Networks and the Federal Government.** 1943

Sadowski, Robert Paul. **An Analysis of Statutory Laws Governing Commercial and Educational Broadcasting in the Fifty States.** *(Doctoral Thesis, The University of Iowa, 1973)* 1979

Schwarzlose, Richard Allen. **The American Wire Services:** A Study of Their Development as a Social Institution. *(Doctoral Thesis, University of Illinois at Urbana-Champaign, 1965)* 1979

Smith, Ralph Lewis. **A Study of the Professional Criticism of Broadcasting in the United States. 1920-1955.** *(Doctoral Thesis, University of Wisconsin, 1959)* 1979

Stamps, Charles Henry. **The Concept of the Mass Audience in American Broadcasting:** An Historical-Descriptive Study. *(Doctoral Dissertation, Northwestern University, 1956)* 1979

Steiner, Peter O. **Workable Competition in the Radio Broadcasting Industry.** *(Doctoral Thesis, Harvard University, 1949)* 1979

Stern, Robert H. **The Federal Communications Commission and Television:** The Regulatory Process in an Environment of Rapid Technical Innovation. *(Doctoral Thesis, Harvard University, 1950)* 1979

Tomlinson, John D. **International Control of Radiocommunications.** 1945

Ulloth, Dana Royal. **The Supreme Court:** A Judicial Review of the Federal Communications Commission. *(Doctoral Dissertation, University of Missouri-Columbia, 1971)* 1979